SEWING on the LINE

Fast & Easy Foundation Piecing

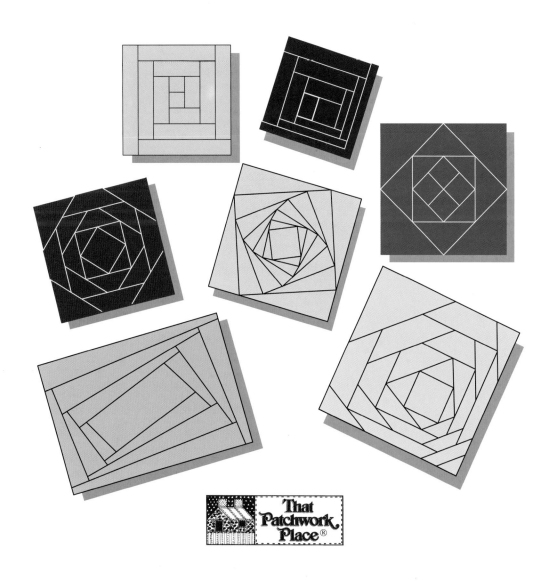

Lesly-Claire Greenberg

DEDICATION/ACKNOWLEDGMENTS

In loving memory of my mother, Laura Miller Cohen, Lenore Parham, and Mary Ann Rush, whose friendships enriched my life.

There are many ways to say thank you for all the encouragement one receives when undertaking a project as large as a book. I am indebted to many people for their pushing and prodding, criticism and praise, pressure and support. To my wonderful family and friends, editors, students, and the quilters who generously loaned their work, *thank you, merci beaucoup, gracias!*

CREDITS

Editor .... Ursula Reikes
Managing Editor .... Greg Sharp
Copy Editor .... Liz McGehee
Text and Cover Design .... Kay Green
Typesetting .... Kay Green
Photography .... Brent Kane
Illustration and Graphics .... Laurel Strand
Stephanie Benson
Laurie Osborn

Sewing on the Line©
©1993 by Lesly-Claire Greenberg

That Patchwork Place, Inc.
PO Box 118
Bothell, WA 98041-0118 USA

Printed in Hong Kong
03 02 01 00 99   6 5 4 3

Greenberg, Lesly-Claire.
    Sewing on the line / Lesly-Claire Greenberg.
        p.   cm.
    ISBN 1-56477-030-3
    1. Quilting—Patterns. 2. Patchwork—Patterns.   I. Title.
TT835.G75   1993
746.46—dc20
93-3601
CIP

CONTENTS

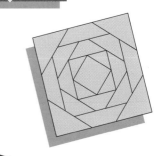

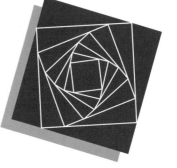

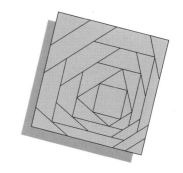

INTRODUCTION

Celtic Cross by Mary Ann Rush, 1992, Fairfax, Virginia, 21" x 21". This quilt variation is made with an Offset Pineapple block that Mary Ann reduced to 2⅜".

Rubber-stamp quiltmaking evolved over a period of time out of my need to create a more precise method of machine piecing. In the late seventies, I was making strip-pieced vests when strip piecing was the new rage. To strip piece, you sewed through the foundation from the top, using the cut edge of the previous strip as a placement guide and the right-hand edge of the presser foot for a seam-allowance guide.

One of my strip-pieced projects was my original pieced vest. Designing this vest was to be my entrance into professional quiltmaking, planning a pattern and class from the very first sketch. The vest turned out beautifully; it was everything that I had envisioned, from its very strange and descriptive armhole notch to the lovely range of purple fabrics. I published my first pattern and began teaching classes; both were well received.

I entered the vest in the National Quilting Association Show; I thought that the audience was ready for something new. The judges disqualified the garment on the grounds that one of the strips on the back was crooked. I was outraged. After all, strip piecing was meant to be fluid. I claimed that it was impossible to strip piece in perfectly straight lines, and I set out to prove it. Instead, I proved that by drawing lines on the wrong side of a block foundation and sewing directly on the lines, not on the strip, I could create a precisely pieced vest requiring a lot less work.

This new direction intrigued me. Perhaps this was a method that could be applied to other designs. It was, so I incorporated it into my new pattern line.

Using a 3½" Log Cabin block, I designed a new vest. After tracing the block on foundation cloth, I completed two blocks, using silk fabrics. They were beautiful and square. After sketching a design with the vest fronts made out of miniature blocks, there was only one way that I would consider piecing the twenty-six blocks that I would need. I traced all the foundations and employed the new rotary cutter for cutting strips; I stayed up all night. When the blocks went together in a snap, I had a wonderful vest and a new class.

The method was an immediate hit. The only complaint was having to trace all those blocks! I still remember one class I taught in Rochester, New York, where a husband came to class and traced the foundations for his wife!

I rejected the idea of printing fabric with my block designs because of the possibility of inaccuracies; the lines and shapes could be distorted when washed. But stamping block designs on fabric foundations, using a rubber stamp and ink, was a natural solution. Besides, I had always liked rubber stamps and had collected them for many years.

I had my first stamps made, but they cost well over fifty dollars each and weren't very durable. Permanent ink ate through the plastic/acrylic in a matter of weeks, removing the numbers and lines. I tried other inks and different kinds of rubber until I hit on the combination that I use today. Gray rubber and laundry ink have worked well for several years and have withstood the test of time.

The Log Cabin rubber stamps worked so well that I began seeing stamps in other shapes and configurations. It was worth drafting and making a stamp for any project that required more than ten blocks. I began producing stamps to sell more Log Cabin Vest patterns. Now I have come to think of the stamp or foundation method as such a creative direction that there is no end to the possibilities.

Using a design grid as a foundation on either fabric or paper produces a high-quality product and frees you to spend more time on planning color and design instead of making templates and tracing designs. Efficiency is always my goal. Do it, do it well, and do it as fast as possible. Using this method, you sew by the numbers; no previous experience is necessary.

My aim is to give the average quilter a chance at being a quilt artist. As students are turned on to color in my color classes and are given the foundations as a tool, I see them producing sketch after sketch of wonderful quilts. These new artists are hungry to experiment with different configurations. I don't think that we have even begun to scratch the surface when it comes to the possible design variations. We are limited only by our imagination, and perhaps, the fabric at hand.

STAMPING SUPPLIES

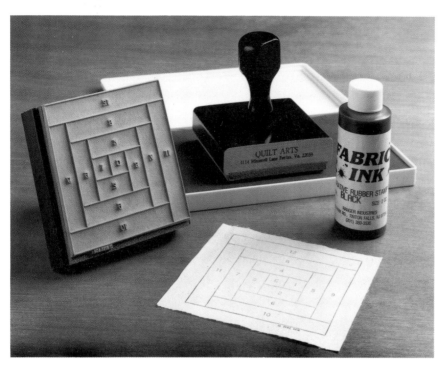

Traditional gray rubber stamps and one brand of solvent-based ink

RUBBER STAMPS

There are several brands of rubber stamps for quiltmaking. (See Resource List on page 87.) Rubber stamps make printing a foundation very simple and quick. Several different types of rubber are used in stamps; each has a different composition and different ink requirements.

The nicest thing about a rubber stamp is that it can make an impression on any surface. Three surfaces fit our needs: fabric, paper, and tear-away stabilizer. Both paper and tear-away foundations are torn away from the completed piecing; fabric remains as an extra layer in the finished project.

Traditional rubber stamps work well with both solvent- and water-based inks. Acrylic rubber stamps are compatible with water-based or acrylic inks. Solvent-based inks will deteriorate the soft see-through acrylic material. Regular inked stamp pads can be used with acrylic/plastic and traditional rubber stamps.

To prolong the life of any stamp, do not leave it sitting on the ink pad or near a source of heat; remove excess ink; avoid getting the wooden block wet.

INKS

Permanent fabric ink is desirable for stamping foundations on cloth. Regular stamp-pad ink can be used for stamping foundations on paper. To avoid any surprises later, I suggest testing any ink that you have not yet tried. (See page 14.)

Fabric inks come in two basic types: solvent-based inks, which do not require heat setting for permanency; and acrylic, water-based inks, which do need to be heat set.

Solvent-based inks smell like alcohol and are permanent on fabric when air dried. They are also permanent on the pad. When not in use, keep the stamp pad tightly closed and sealed in an air-tight plastic bag.

Acrylic stamping ink and paint can also be used to prepare block foundations. This type of ink needs to be heat set with an iron. Read the label information that comes with your ink. When using acrylic inks, make a disposable pad from a square of felt on a plastic plate, then store it in a zippered plastic bag in the refrigerator. It will keep for several days. Acrylic ink is the only permanent ink that, to my knowledge, will not cause the deterioration of acrylic stamps. Clean up with soap and water and avoid getting the wooden stamp mounts wet.

STAMP PADS

Choose a felt stamp pad large enough to accommodate your largest stamp. If you use only miniature stamps, a regular-sized pad will do. A felt pad usually has a piece of cloth wrapped around the felt. A foam pad will deteriorate rapidly if used with solvent-based inks.

To ink an uninked pad:

Shake the ink well and use a small brush, or the applicator if one is supplied, to apply ink to the area of the pad that will be used. Never pour the ink on the pad; it will make a mess. Be sparing with the ink; let it sink into the felt before you begin.

Firmly press the stamp on the pad; if the ink gurgles and sputters, wait a few moments and let the ink sink in. Firmly press the stamp onto the foundation material. If the impression is not complete, try layering your foundation material. I generally stamp on four to six layers of foundation cloth or a pad of paper for a better impression.

When you finish stamping, wrap the closed pad in a zippered plastic bag; it will stay moist for several days. Wrap your brush also. Clean your hands with solvent or alcohol.

A Touch of Yellow by Leslie Pfeifer, 1991, Fairfax, Virginia, 16½" x 16½". This quilt uses a 3" Offset Pineapple block.

QUILTING MATERIALS & SUPPLIES

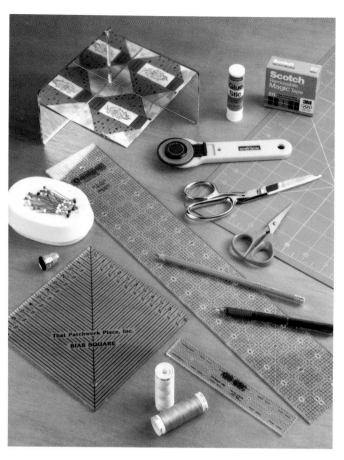

Needles: I prefer a lightweight needle for hand sewing in a size 10 or 12. For machine sewing, I use a fine to medium needle (70/80), with a sharp point.

Thread: I use silk-finished cotton (Swiss Metrosene) for hand piecing, and machine embroidery thread in a neutral color for machine piecing.

Generally speaking, use dark thread for dark fabrics, and light thread for light fabrics. However, I find that using black thread literally obliterates the foundation lines, making piecing more difficult. Neutral gray is unobtrusive and visually less stressful. In the bobbin, use any color that blends with the pieced fabric. This is a good way to use up all your half-filled bobbins.

Pins: I use Iris super-fine steel pins, with their tiny heads and 1½"-long shafts, for general hand and machine piecing. I prefer large, white-headed pins for machine piecing when the blocks and rows are joined and when sewing through thick layers. T-pins are great for securing blocks on a design board.

Iron: You must have an iron close by. Choose one with a steam feature that can be turned on and off. If you use paper foundations, steam will make the paper curl and that can be very frustrating.

Ironing Board: I like to use my adjustable-height, full-size ironing board as a surface for stamping. It can be raised higher than table height, making it easier on your back. Many of my students work with an ironing pad, a travel ironing board, or an empty fabric bolt wrapped in flannel.

Fabric: A good selection of fabric is always essential, but this should not limit a beginner from taking part in the fun of foundation piecing. Scraps are very useful. You need very little of any one fabric to complete most of the projects in this book. Check the remnant and scrap bins and collect ¼-yard pieces in a variety of prints. Use lots of different prints.

Preshrink all cotton fabrics. Wash in the washer and use detergent to remove the sizing so you can control the fabric. If a fabric decides to be the boss, please consider discarding it to avoid confrontations later. Yardage requirements in this book are based on 40 usable inches after preshrinking.

I work primarily with 100% cotton fabrics. When using muslin foundations for support, you can also use a variety of fashion fabrics, such as lamé, silk, and velvet. Fabric clubs advertised in sewing magazines are a good source of fashion fabric swatches, often large enough to complete small projects.

Muslin: High-quality muslin is an absolute necessity for hand piecing as well as for machine piecing. If you mark your foundations on muslin instead of paper, you can sew your project by hand or by machine, or use a combination of both.

Tracing Paper: Thin tracing or parchment paper makes a good foundation for machine piecing. The paper is removed from the finished piecing, and the pieced top can easily be hand quilted.

Tear-Away Stabilizer: Tear-away stabilizer is a nonwoven fabric made of synthetic fibers so it acts like paper in foundation piecing.

Transfer Pencil: A transfer pencil can be used to easily and inexpensively duplicate foundations. Transfer pencils and pens are available in several different colors. Test the color before you use it in your final quilt.

Mechanical Pencil: You can use a mechanical pencil with a fine point to trace foundations on fabric or paper. A medium lead, HB, works well with minimal smearing.

Victorian Dream by Jasmine Moghissi, 1992, Vienna, Virginia, 16" x 16". Jasmine used the 3" Log Cabin Twist block and three fabrics to piece the sixteen blocks.

Rotary Cutter: This tool with a circular blade that revolves like a pizza cutter makes cutting multiple strips very simple, and it saves busy hands from repetitive injuries and strain that often result from cutting with scissors. They are also great time-savers. You must use a cutting mat with a rotary cutter. (See page 10.) Be sure to change your blade when it shows signs of dulling. A dull blade means that you have to press harder, and the harder you have to press, the less control you have. It also causes unwanted strain on your arm and wrist. This is a precision instrument that requires respect. Close the safety cover after each cut, before you lay the cutter down.

Rotary cutters come in two sizes, 1" and 1¾". The larger size is more versatile because you can cut several layers at once.

Cutting Mat: Rotary cutting mats are made of durable plastic, similar in nature to vinyl or linoleum. Mats are self healing and come in a variety of sizes. My work surface accommodates the largest size, 20" x 30". I carry a 9" x 12" when I am teaching or traveling. A small 6" x 8" cutting mat resides near my sewing machine. Grid lines can be helpful in lining up fabric for strip cutting. Many rotary-cutting mats are green, but there are also translucent white cutting mats that can be used on a light box.

The composition of the cutting mats makes them susceptible to extremes in temperature. Store flat whenever possible; keep away from hot irons, hot lamps, hot light boxes, hot cars, and hot hamburgers. My first cutting mat was destroyed when I left it on the table under the slide sorter.

Cutting Guides: Cutting guides are clear acrylic "rulers" and are approximately ⅛" thick. For cutting strips, choose a ruler at least 3" wide and 12" long (wide enough to cut strips 3" wide and long enough to accommodate 44"-wide fabric, folded into fourths). I also like to have a small square handy for trimming completed blocks. The 6" square works well with my 6" x 8" cutting mat and is very transportable.

Keep your acrylic rulers away from heat; don't leave them in a hot car!

Masking Tape: Use 2"-wide masking tape when making fabric mock-ups of your quilt blocks. (See page 71.) Fabric swatches with tape on the back are more stable and can be glued to paper with a glue stick. The edges of the swatches remain neat for a long time without fraying. Place the tape on the wrong side of the fabric before cutting the swatches.

Glue Stick: Only use a glue stick that is recommended for paper or cloth. Don't use any glue that is runny or gooey; it will only frustrate you and make a mess, too. When gluing mock-ups, put the glue on the paper, not on the fabric.

Removable Transparent Tape: This tape has sticking powers similar to Post-it™ Notes. It can be useful in place of pins when sewing on paper foundations, and it can be reused many times.

Peppermint Twist by Mary Ann Rush, 1992, Fairfax, Virginia, 13" x 13". Mary Ann used a variation of the 3" Log Cabin Twist block by leaving off the last round of strips.

Photocopier: Access to a photocopier is convenient when designing blocks and quilts. It is a good way to make reproductions of your block for fabric mock-ups. You can also enlarge designs to try them in different sizes. When you want to investigate a new size, produce your foundations from the photocopy, using any of the methods described on pages 13–16.

Mirrors: Two small, square mirrors, held at a 90° angle along the edge of your square, can help you visualize repeats of your block without sewing additional blocks.

Computer Quilt Program: A quilt design program is extremely useful for imagining finished quilts without ever sewing. It's great for coloring blocks and repeating them in different configurations. Be careful, though. This is easily the best video game in town; it's difficult to tear yourself away, even if you are not a video enthusiast.

Japanese Pineapple by Mary Ann Rush, 1991, Fairfax, Virginia, 26″ x 26″. This quilt is pieced with a 6″ variation of a Pineapple block.

Miscellaneous Supplies: In my area, "Adaptive Aquatics" is taught at the local recreation center. This water-exercise class is for the physically challenged. Quilters physically abuse themselves in contortions of all sorts to get the perfect quilting stitch, so I call my quilting class "Adaptive Quilting." I am constantly searching for ways to make our art more comfortable, physically as well as mentally.

A spoon for hand quilting, used in your underneath hand, protects your fingers from constant pricking. This is important if you wear contact lenses; scabby fingers do not handle delicate lenses well. It is also very important if you have received radiation treatments or have had lymph-node surgery for breast cancer. It can be devastating to be told that you can't quilt because you could get an infection too easily. Thanks to a spoon underneath, many of our friends can still enjoy quilting.

A lap frame on a stand helps keep your posture relaxed. You do not have to bend and contort to wedge the hoop in between you and the table. My favorite frame was made for me by a friend's husband. His design is so comfortable that he has been coerced into making them for our local shop. Sam is not looking for another career; he has several already, but every time I teach "Adaptive Quilting," we sell out. I bless both Sue and Sam whenever I sit down to quilt.

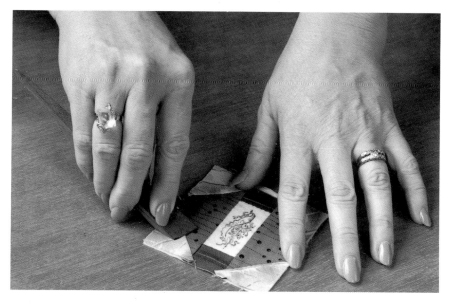

A wooden iron helps in finger pressing.

Finger cots are used in medical applications, but you'll love using one of these little rubber sheaths on the forefinger of your quilting hand. This little piece of latex will protect your finger against blisters that result from grasping the needle, a condition that can be painful. I prefer a finger cot to using a rubber disk for the same purpose, as the disk must be picked up after each stitch.

A new gadget that I recently acquired is called a wooden iron. It is handmade and probably had its origin in the Orient. This wooden iron is used for finger pressing seams, an absolute delight with the rubber-stamp technique. It is not only handy with all those seams, but it saves your fingernail from the repeated pressure of finger pressing.

The telephone is a real friend when you are home with your quilting. Companionship gets us through some of the low points of the day and is a pleasant break from work, whether your primary work is in the home, office, or other setting. Quilting with friends, as in the quilting bee, is an old tradition, but often our busy lives don't allow much time for it. The telephone has filled in the gap. Unfortunately, there are many craftspeople walking around complaining of neckaches, backaches, and other related ailments, such as cauliflower ear. I think you can trace many of these complaints to the telephone. If you need to take care of your phoning while you sew, invest in a headset. Select one that has the features you want and make sure that it is comfortable and doesn't leave you with a headache. While writing, I have found myself with the headset on when I wasn't even talking—I never know when the phone will ring.

Speaking of a ringing phone, did you know that answering machines have a little feature called call screening, which allows you to listen to the caller before you decide to answer the phone? Most telemarketeers never leave a message. That can save you from answering the phone several times in one sitting.

PRODUCING FOUNDATIONS

There are several ways to produce foundations on which to sew. The grid that you will "print" on the right side of the foundation is the mirror image of your final pieced block; you will place the strips on the wrong side of the foundation and stitch from the right side. See "Sewing Logs," pages 19–20, for more information on the stitching process.

A word of caution is in order here. From the methods listed below, choose only one method to produce the foundations for your project. Different techniques produce foundations that might vary slightly in size.

Before you produce foundations, you must choose paper (or tear-away stabilizer) or cloth. There are pros and cons for both.

The backs of "Over Under" and "Interweave Too." One quilt utilizes muslin foundations with hand sewing; the other uses paper foundations with machine sewing.

Cloth can be sewn by hand or machine. Changing back and forth from hand to machine stitching is easy with fabric foundations and makes your project very portable. If you need to remove stitching, the fabric foundation stays in one piece and can be used again. The disadvantage to using cloth foundations is that they remain in the finished project, adding weight and making hand quilting more difficult because of the extra layer. In addition, stamping on fabric requires permanent ink.

Tracing paper (or tear-away stabilizer) is easy to use for foundations because you can see through it, making placement a cinch. Because the foundation is removed after piecing, very little ink remains in contact with the quilt, making it possible to use a regular inked stamp pad. You can hand quilt the finished piece.

If you use paper foundations, you cannot piece by hand. And, if you must remove inaccurately stitched pieces, there's a good chance the paper won't survive the ripping. Also, all the foundation material must be removed before quilting.

Sewing on the Vine by Leslie Pfeifer, 1992, Fairfax, Virginia, 16" x 16". Leslie used a 3½" Pineapple block in traditional colors, then appliquéd a vine in the outer border.

STAMPING ON FABRIC

Before stamping on fabric, it is a good idea to test an unfamiliar ink for washability first. I prefer a permanent ink that will not run later and leave smeared ink on the finished quilt. Some quilters have used regular ink pads successfully, but I don't recommend this practice; I fear that the ink might reappear later, much like the marks from "disappearing-ink" markers have!

To test inks, stamp a block on the foundation material that you are planning to use. (It saves time to test ink on all possible materials at the same time. When testing on paper or tear-away stabilizer, remove a portion of the foundation before washing.) Make sample blocks, using all-white fabric. Then using soap or detergent in the water, wash gently and dry quickly in the dryer, or spread out on a protected, flat surface to dry. The soap or detergent that you use and the mineral content of your water could affect the results of the testing. Once you have found an ink that does not run, you're ready to produce the number of foundation blocks you need for your quilt.

Cut the foundation cloth, preferably a high-quality muslin, into strips the width of the stamp, plus 1". This size easily accommodates the stamp and allows for margins that make it easy to handle the foundation. Cut across the width of the muslin. Then layer the strips neatly on the ironing board, pressing them smooth as you layer them. This provides a nice pad of muslin on which to stamp, and it compensates for any minor warping that might occur in a wooden-mounted stamp. When each strip is stamped, hang it over the arm of a lamp or chair to dry overnight.

STAMPING ON PAPER & TEAR-AWAY STABILIZER

The stamping procedure is similar on paper and tear-away stabilizer. Because the paper or stabilizer foundation is torn away from the finished piecing, very little ink remains in contact with the finished block. Choose an inked pad in a color that you can see. I have had success with black ink pads from several of the traditional office-supply stores. You could choose any color that you have on hand. If you are unsure of the ink, perform a little test. (See page 14.)

Stamp firmly on the tracing paper or stabilizer. I prefer to leave the paper on the pad. Leave about an inch between each impression and let them dry thoroughly before using. Drying takes only a few minutes.

TRACING

You can trace block designs directly onto fabric or paper. This method is useful when only a few foundations are needed. Of course, it is a test of patience to see how many you can trace; thirty seems to be the upper limits for most of us.

To trace on fabric, tape the original block design to your work table. Tape the muslin foundation fabric in place over the design. Trace all the lines of the design, using a ruler with ⅛", ¼", or ½" grid lines as an aid. Print the numbers and letters that appear on the design. You can also use a small light box or a window for a work table if you can't see the design through the muslin.

Tracing on paper is very easy. Follow the same procedure as for fabric. Use a fine-line black marker for better visibility.

Tracing block designs is the best way to produce foundations in larger sizes. You can use tracing to add logs to smaller stamped or printed foundations to make blocks larger. You can also enlarge blocks on a photocopier, then trace as many as you need.

USING TRANSFER PENCILS AND PENS

Trace your design onto paper as directed in the instructions accompanying your transfer pencil or pen. When you create an iron-on transfer of a block design and print it on the foundation fabric, you get a mirror-image of the original. Because you sew from the wrong side, the finished block will be the same as the original design. This method produces foundations that are the opposite direction of the other methods and could present a problem with some designs, such as Virginia Reel or any other twisting design. The finished quilt design could twist in the opposite direction of your quilt plan. Be sure to keep this in mind if you plan to use more than one method to produce foundations for a project.

PHOTOCOPYING

You can photocopy designs to produce foundations. However, I find this the least satisfactory method as photocopy machines tend to distort the designs in one direction more than another. If I am producing paper foundations, I prefer to use a see-through tracing paper as it is more difficult to see through opaque paper like that used in a copier. I have seen quilters copying directly onto muslin, but it could damage the copier and might be messy when the dry ink and toner flakes off.

Be sure to make as many copies as you need on the same photocopier. This way, any distortion to the design should be the same on all the copies. Always make photocopies from the original design; do not make photocopies from previously photocopied designs. Distortion increases with each subsequent generation of photocopies.

Commercially printed foundations are now available at many quilt shops for many different designs.

Japanese Lanterns by Mary Ann Rush, 1992, Fairfax, Virginia, 19¼" x 23½". Mary Ann drafted her 6" block on tracing paper. This block is a variation of the 3" Offset Pineapple block.

COLOR

Color is an important factor in any quilt project, no matter which design you choose to make. With so many small pieces in these blocks, there is room to utilize a large palette of colors. Try using tiny pieces of contrasting hues for sparkle. Blend a palette from the darkest to the lightest. The wider the color range you use, the fuller and richer the finished work.

Keep in mind the basic color harmonies that you may have learned in color theory. If color theory isn't your bag, choose a fabric that has the feeling you want. If you like a fabric, then it is a good starting point for a project. Don't worry if you decide to discard the very one you chose first. Starting is half the battle, and the first fabric chosen has served its place in the color auditioning. Sometimes, the first fabric chosen ends up blending in too well with the pieced work. If you discard it from the piecing but still want to use it, consider it for the backing or the lining of your project.

To avoid confusion in placing fabrics, make a color mock-up or identification chart to use as a reference guide when working with complicated blocks.

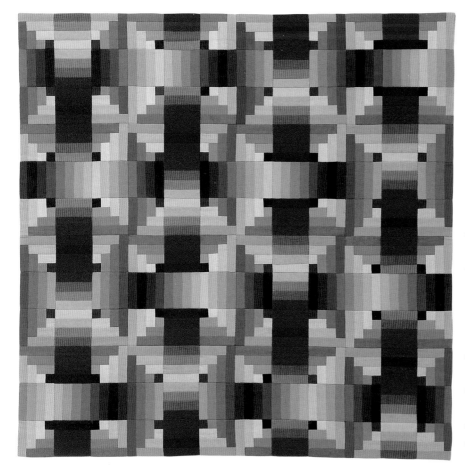

Over Under Variation, Interweave Too by Lesly-Claire Greenberg, 1992, Fairfax, Virginia, 36" x 36". This quilt is a larger variation of the project quilt on page 34. Lesly-Claire used two different hand-dyed gradations to make the woven ribbons and two different gradations for the blocks. It differs from the project on page 34 in the sequence and placement of the gradations, using four color ranges.

Sewing on the Line

Cutting Strips and Logs

Prepare the block foundations, using one of the methods described on pages 13–16, and select fabrics. The following sample blocks illustrate the basic steps for sewing on the line.

I cut the majority of my strips 1" wide, even though ¾" is adequate in many cases. It's so frustrating to pick up a narrow strip, carefully place and sew it, only to find out that the strip is too narrow and must be replaced.

Cut strips from selected fabrics, ½" wider than the finished dimensions of the "logs" in the foundation. Then cut strips into lengths, ½" (two ¼"-wide seam allowances) longer than the finished "logs." When estimating the lengths to cut the strips for tiny "logs," you really need only a ⅛"-wide seam allowance at each end, or a total of ¼", but you may wish to allow a full ¼"-wide seam allowance in small applications until you are comfortable with this technique.

It is also acceptable to sew logs using longer strips, but I find that the weight of the strip tends to make the logs shift off course. Although you might waste a little fabric by cutting the strips into approximate lengths, I think it is well worth the effort. *The dimensions given for cutting logs in each of the quilt projects in this book include necessary seam allowances.*

Remember, all the measurements given in the projects are guides. You can measure precisely if you are more comfortable doing so. Because sewing on the line provides a precise sewing line, precise cutting is not really important as long as the strips cut are larger than the guides.

Monet I by Lesly-Claire Greenberg, 1992, Fairfax, Virginia, approximately 45" x 35". This quilt variation was made with the Rectangle Twist block.

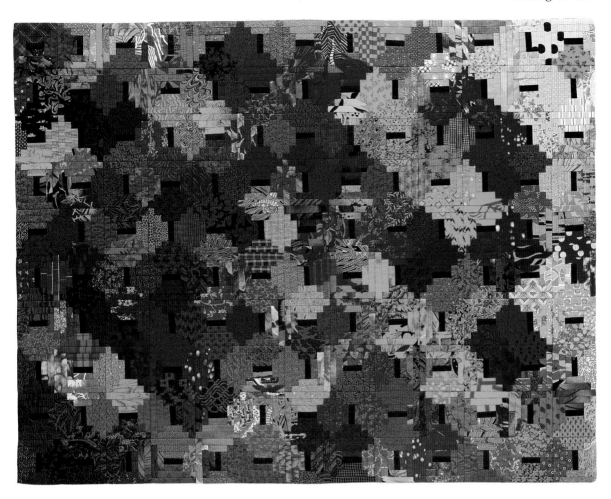

SEWING LOGS

There are three very simple rules to follow when using a prepared foundation for sewing on the line.

1. All marked lines are sewing lines.
2. All fabric strips are positioned for stitching on the unmarked side of the foundation.
3. If you have to trim previously sewn "logs" to place the next "log," turn the block over. Fold the foundation back, out of the way, on the next line that you are going to sew, and trim, leaving no less than ⅛"-wide seam allowances.

Before you make the sample blocks to learn this new technique, there are some additional cutting and stitching rules you should know.

1. When cutting strips for the logs, add ¼"-wide seam allowances for logs that will finish to ½" or wider. For example, cut 1"-wide strips for ½"-wide finished logs.
2. The grain of the fabric is not critical in these small logs. The only time a crooked grain will show up is when a striped or plaid fabric is used. When using fabric foundations, all logs are stabilized.
3. When sewing by machine on the marked lines, begin a stitch or two before the line and continue a stitch or two beyond the end of the line. It is not necessary to backstitch, since the stitches will be secured by the next line of sewing.

Flower Drum Song by Lesly-Claire Greenberg, 1990, Fairfax, Virginia, 31½" x 25". This quilt was pieced with a 2⅝" Courthouse Steps block. For instructions to make this quilt, see page 63.

Set the stitch length at 12–15 stitches per inch when using a fabric foundation. Set the stitch length for 15–20 stitches per inch when using a paper foundation. The smaller stitches make it easier to remove the paper.

4. When sewing by hand on the marked lines, begin and end the stitching on the line. Be careful not to pull the thread too tightly as you sew. If you do, the block will pucker.

5. After adding each log, finger press the log open over the space it is to cover on the foundation. Hold it up to the light to make sure that an adequate seam allowance extends into the adjacent areas. Then turn the foundation over and trim any excess seam allowance to eliminate unnecessary bulk.

6. On most Log Cabin blocks and their variations, the first "log" you place will cover the area marked C (center). On other blocks, you will begin with log #1. Then you will add the remaining logs in numerical order until the foundation is completely covered.

   After adding each log, finger press the log into position on the foundation. Secure the log with a pin, if necessary, to keep it fully open and flat while you add the next log.

7. Press the completed block, then trim to square up the edges, leaving a ¼"-wide seam allowance beyond the outer line of the printed design on the foundation.

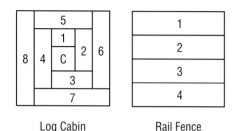

Log Cabin   Rail Fence

SAMPLE BLOCKS

Before you make any of the projects in this book, I recommend that you make a sample of each of the following blocks to learn the technique and perfect your "sewing on the line."

RAIL FENCE

The starting point on the Rail Fence block is log #1.

1. Place log #1 on the unmarked side of the foundation, right side up, then place log #2 on top of log #1, with right sides facing. Hold the foundation up to the light (or use a light table) to make sure that the pieces cover the area marked #1 and that they extend by the width of a seam allowance beyond all the lines around the area marked #1.

2. While carefully holding the logs in place, turn the foundation over and sew on the line between log #1 and log #2.

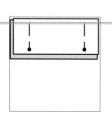

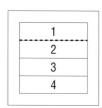

3. Finger press log #2 open over the area marked #2. Hold the foundation up to the light to make sure that the edges of log #1 and log #2 extend beyond the printed lines of the foundation. Pin, if necessary, to keep the log open.

4. Complete the design by adding logs #3 and #4 in the same manner. Press the completed block and trim the edges, leaving a ¼"-wide seam allowance beyond the outer line of the printed square of the foundation.

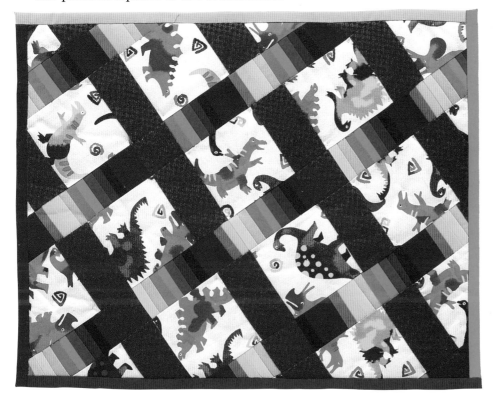

Baby Doll Brights by Kathleen Kurke, 1992, Fairfax, Virginia, 18" x 23". This doll quilt was made for Kathleen's niece, using the collection of colorwheel solids accumulated in a color class. The quilt variation uses the 2" Rail Fence block, larger squares, and strips.

LOG CABIN

1. Place the center square on the unmarked side of the foundation, right side up. Hold the foundation up to the light (or use a light table) and make sure that the fabric center covers the area on the foundation marked C. Be sure that fabric extends past the center area. There should be a ¼"-wide seam allowance extending beyond all four lines around C into the adjacent areas.

   Place log #1 right side down over the center square. Hold up to the light to make sure that it extends into the area marked #1 and beyond both ends of the area marked #1.

2. Turn foundation over while carefully holding the logs in place and sew on the line between log #1 and the center.

3. Finger press log #1 open over the area marked #1. Pin, if necessary, to keep the log open.

4. Place log #2 across log #1 and the center, with right sides facing. Turn foundation over while carefully holding the logs in place and sew on the line between log #2 and log #1/center.

5. Continue to add logs in numerical order to complete the design. Press the completed block and trim edges, leaving a ¼"-wide seam allowance beyond the outer line of the printed square on the foundation.

I Thought I Saw a Drunkard by Nancy J. Jacoby, 1992, Wabash, Indiana, 15" x 15". This quilt was made with a variation on the 3" Offset Log Cabin. Nancy has an additional log on the thin side of the block. This layout is from a book by Pepper Cory.

PINEAPPLE

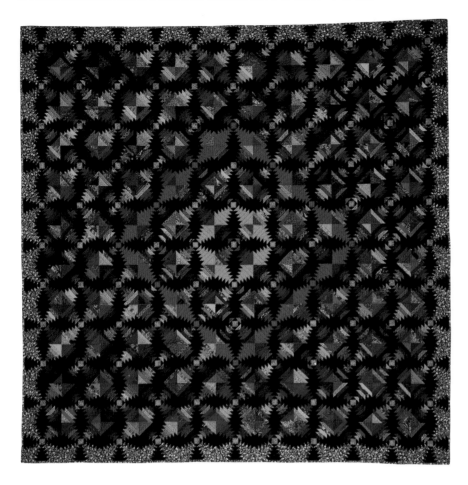

Pineapple Quilt by Barbara Dean, 1991, Chantilly, Virginia, 100" x 100". This king-size quilt variation was pieced with 9" printed Pineapple blocks.

1. Place the center square on the unmarked side of the foundation over the area marked C. Make sure that edges extend into the adjacent areas. Place log #1 on top of the center, with right sides facing.

2. While carefully holding logs in place, turn foundation over and sew on the line between the center and log #1.

3. Finger press log #1 open over the area marked #1. Add logs #2, #3, and #4.

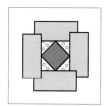

4. The next four logs are sewn at a 45° angle to the sewing line you just finished. Trim previously sewn logs to make placing the next round of logs easier. (See rule #3, page 19.)

5. Continue adding logs in numerical order until the design is completed. Press completed blocks and trim to square up edges, leaving a ¼"-wide seam allowance beyond the outer line of the marked square on the foundation.

ASSEMBLING BLOCKS INTO A QUILT

1. Arrange your finished blocks as desired or follow a specific quilt plan.
2. To join the blocks into rows, place blocks with right sides together, matching the outer lines on the marked square of both blocks. Pin corners and along the outer line. Be sure pins are placed on the outer lines of both blocks. Sew on the line.

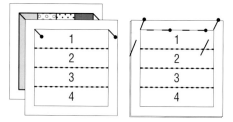

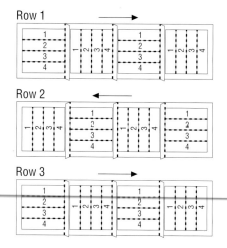

3. Press the seams of alternate rows in opposite directions.

4. Join rows, making sure to match the seams between each block. Place pins at each intersection and along the outer lines of the marked squares. Sew on the line.

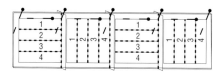

5. Press seams open to reduce bulk. Long seams can be pressed toward one side if the fabrics are not bulky.

PREPARING KITS

I find it helpful to prepare foundations and cut the strips for several blocks at a time. Then I place each set in its own zippered plastic bag so I can take it along to work on while waiting in line, sitting at the dentist's office, or waiting for my family when they choose to ride the big roller coaster at the amusement park (and I don't). You might find it a time-saver, too, even if you plan to machine piece your blocks.

Preparing kits is easy with Log Cabin and Log Cabin variations. The basic Log Cabin is made of lights on one side of the block and darks on the other, divided on the diagonal. In the block illustrated at right, twelve logs surround the center square. When cutting logs for this block, I like to use the same fabric (a light) for logs #1 and #2, and the same fabric (a dark) for logs #3 and #4. This repeats around the block, using new fabrics in each round of logs (light or dark, depending on the location in the block). In the block shown, I used one color for the center and three lights and three darks for the logs.

Of course, there are other ways to color Log Cabin blocks, but this is comfortable and eliminates confusion, especially if you are new to this method. It minimizes agonizing over fabric placement for each and every log and saves a lot of time.

When I cut logs for a Log Cabin quilt, I select all the fabrics for my color story, then divide them into darks and lights (or two different colors, such as pink and green). Then I layer the color groups for cutting, limiting the number of layers to no more than six for accuracy and ease in cutting. Next, I cut the layers into strips of the appropriate widths. Last, I cut the strips into logs of the required lengths. Be sure to cut the longer logs first, as you can often get the smaller ones from the scraps remaining from cutting the longer logs.

After all the logs have been cut, I lay out the prepared foundations and deal out the required sets of light and dark logs. It's a lot like playing cards. Once I've "dealt" the center, logs #1 and #2 and logs #3 and #4 (round 1), I sidestep the next two foundations and continue dealing the next round. From this point on, I do this sidestepping for each set of two logs, as it is the key to getting as much random placement in the blocks as possible—without agonizing over it or thinking too hard.

When the dealing is over, I look at each set of logs to discover any fabric duplications within blocks. These I fix by exchanging the duplicate logs for another set of logs of a different fabric in the correct lengths.

One last thing to remember: The more fabrics you choose at the outset, the more variation you will have in your finished blocks.

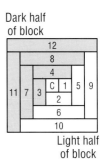

Dark half
of block

Light half
of block

Foundation Block

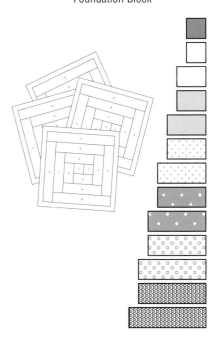

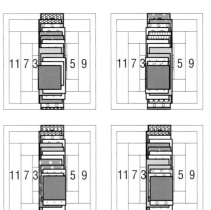

PROJECTS

RAIL FENCE

Quilt Size: 12" x 12"

Finished Block: 2"

Use 2" Rail Fence block template on page 67.

1
2
3
4

Rail Fence

MATERIALS
44"-wide fabric

16 Rail Fence foundations

Fabric A (bright) ⅛ yd.
Fabric B (light) ⅛ yd.
Fabric C (medium) ⅛ yd.
Fabric D (dark) ⅛ yd.
Border ⅛ yd.
Backing ⅜ yd.

Rail Fence, designed by Lesly-Claire Greenberg, 1992, Fairfax, Virginia, 12" x 12". Blocks pieced by Becky Molitor.

CUTTING

Cut all strips across the fabric width (crosswise grain).

Cut 1"-wide strips and then logs, following the chart below.

Fabric	Number of Strips	Log Number	Log Length	Number of Logs
A	1	1	2½"	16
B	1	2	2½"	16
C	1	3	2½"	16
D	1	4	2½"	16

DIRECTIONS

If you have not made a sample block before starting this quilt, make one now, referring to Sewing on the Line, beginning on page 18.

Rail Fence Piecing

Make 16 Rail Fence blocks, following the piecing directions below.

1. Place log #1, right side up, on the unmarked side of the foundation. Hold the foundation up to the light and make sure log #1 covers the area marked #1.
2. Place log #2 on top of log #1, with right sides together. Hold the foundation up to the light to make sure that log #1 and log #2 cover the area marked #1, and extend the width of a seam allowance on all sides.
3. Turn the foundation over while carefully holding the logs in place and sew on the line between log #1 and log #2.
4. Finger press log #2 open. Pin, if necessary, to keep log open and flat.
5. Add log #3 and log #4 in the same manner.
6. Press completed block and trim to square up edges, leaving a ¼"-wide seam allowance beyond the outer line of the marked square.

Quilt Top Assembly

1. Arrange blocks, as shown in the photo on page 26. Pin blocks into 4 rows of 4 blocks each, matching the outer lines of the marked square and sew on the line. Press seams of alternate rows in opposite directions.
2. Join rows, making sure to match the seams between each block. Press seams open.
3. Cut 2 strips, each 2½" x 8½", and 2 strips, each 2½" x 12½", for the borders. Sew the 8½" strips to opposite sides of the quilt top. Sew the 12½" strips to the remaining sides of the quilt top.

Finishing

1. Cut backing and batting the same size as the quilt top.
2. To finish with the stitch-and-turn method, place batting on the wrong side of the quilt top, then place quilt top on backing, with right sides together. Sew around the edges, leaving an opening on one side for turning. Clip corners and turn right side out.
3. Blindstitch the opening closed; quilt as desired.

Note: *You may finish the quilt in the traditional manner if you prefer. Layer the quilt top with batting and backing and quilt as desired. Finish the edges with binding.*

LOG CABIN PLACE MAT

Place Mat Size: 10½" x 14"

Finished Block: 3½"

Use 3½" Log Cabin block template on page 67.

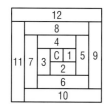

Log Cabin

MATERIALS
44"-wide fabric

For 4 place mats, you will need: 48 Log Cabin foundations

Center ⅛ yd.
#1 Light ⅛ yd.
#2 Light ¼ yd.
#3 Light ⅓ yd.
#1 Dark ⅛ yd.
#2 Dark ¼ yd.
#3 Dark ½ yd.
Backing ½ yd.
Binding ½ yd.

Note: *If you want to make only one place mat, you will need 12 Log Cabin foundations and scraps of light and dark fabrics.*

Log Cabin Place Mat by Lesly-Claire Greenberg, 1992, Fairfax, Virginia, 10½" x 14".

CUTTING

Cut all strips across the fabric width (crosswise grain).

Cut 1"-wide strips and then logs, following the chart below.

CUTTING CHART FOR FOUR PLACE MATS				
Fabric	**Number of Strips**	**Log Number**	**Log Length**	**Number of Logs**
light or dark	2	Center	1"	48
#1 light	3	1	1"	48
		2	1½"	48
#1 dark	5	3	1½"	48
		4	2"	48
#2 light	6	5	2"	48
		6	2½"	48
#2 dark	7	7	2½"	48
		8	3"	48
#3 light	9	9	3"	48
		10	3½"	48
#3 dark	10	11	3½"	48
		12	4"	48

DIRECTIONS

If you have not made a sample block before starting the place mats, make one now, referring to Sewing on the Line, beginning on page 18.

Log Cabin Piecing

Make 12 Log Cabin blocks for each place mat, following the piecing directions below.

1. Place the center square, right side up, on the unmarked side of the foundation. Hold the foundation up to the light and make sure the center square covers the area marked C.
2. Place log #1 on top of the center square, with right sides together. Hold the foundation up to the light and make sure log #1 and the center square cover the area marked C and extend the width of a seam allowance on all sides.
3. Turn the foundation over while carefully holding the logs in place; sew on the line between C and log #1.
4. Finger press log #1 open. Pin, if necessary, to keep log open and flat.
5. Add log #2 in the same way. Sew on the line between log #2 and log #1/C. Finger press log #2 and pin, if necessary, to keep log open and flat.
6. Continue adding logs in numerical order until the block is completed. Remember: logs #1 and #2 are light; logs #3 and #4 are dark; logs #5 and #6 are light; logs #7 and #8 are dark, and so on.
7. Press completed block and trim to square up edges, leaving a ¼"-wide seam allowance beyond the outer line of the marked square.

Place Mat Assembly

1. Arrange blocks into 3 rows of 4 blocks each, as shown in the photo on page 28, or create your own design. Pin the blocks together, matching the outer lines of the marked squares and sew on the line. Press the seams of alternate rows in opposite directions.
2. Join rows, making sure to match the seams between each block. Press seams open.

Finishing

1. Cut a backing the same size as the place mat. Pin backing to place mat with wrong sides together. Add a layer of thin batting or interfacing between the top and backing for a firmer place mat, if desired.
2. Bind the edges.

LOG CABIN PINCUSHION

Pincushion Size: 4" x 4"

Finished Block: 2"

Use 2" Log Cabin block template on page 67.

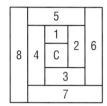

MATERIALS
44"-wide fabric

4 Log Cabin foundations

Scraps of fabric in lights and darks

5" x 5" square of fabric for back of pincushion

Fiberfill or other stuffing material for pincushion

Log Cabin Pincushions by Lesly-Claire Greenberg, 4" x 4".

CUTTING

For the center logs, cut 4 squares, each 1" x 1", from a light or a dark fabric. Cut ⅞"-wide strips for all remaining logs, following the chart below.

Fabric	Number of Strips	Log Number	Log Length	Number of Logs
light 1	1	1	1"	4
		2	1¼"	4
dark 1	1	3	1¼"	4
		4	1¾"	4
light 2	1	5	1¾"	4
		6	2"	4
dark 2	1	7	2"	4
		8	2½"	4

DIRECTIONS

If you have not made a sample block before starting this pincushion, make one now, referring to Sewing on the Line, beginning on page 18.

Log Cabin Piecing

Make 4 Log Cabin blocks, following the piecing directions below.

1. Place the center square, right side up, on the unmarked side of the foundation. Hold the foundation up to the light and make sure the center square covers the area marked C with enough fabric for seam allowance on all sides.
2. Place log #1 on top of the center square, with right sides together. Hold the foundation up to the light to be sure that log #1 and the center square cover the area marked C and extend the width of a seam allowance into adjacent areas.
3. Turn the foundation over while carefully holding the logs in place; sew on the line between C and log #1.
4. Finger press log #1 open. Pin, if necessary, to keep log open and flat.
5. Continue to add logs in numerical order.
6. Press completed block and trim to square up the edges, leaving a ¼"-wide seam allowance beyond the outer line of the marked square.

Pincushion Assembly

1. Arrange 4 blocks in a square, rotating the blocks to create a pleasing balance of color. Sew 2 blocks together, matching the outer lines of the marked squares. Sew the second pair of blocks together. Press the seams of each row in opposite directions.
2. Join pairs of blocks together, making sure to match the seams between the blocks.

Finishing

1. Cut backing fabric the same size as the pincushion top; pin the backing to the pincushion top, with right sides facing.
2. Sew on the outer lines of the marked square, leaving a small opening for turning on one side. Clip corners and turn right side out.
3. Stuff the pincushion firmly with fiberfill, then blindstitch the opening closed.

Enjoy your little gem!

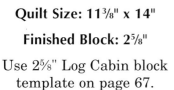

MINIATURE LOG CABIN

Quilt Size: 11⅜" x 14"

Finished Block: 2⅝"

Use 2⅝" Log Cabin block template on page 67.

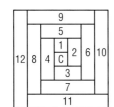

Log Cabin

MATERIALS
44"-wide fabric

12 Log Cabin foundations

Scraps of light and dark fabrics

Border ¼ yd.
Backing ⅓ yd.

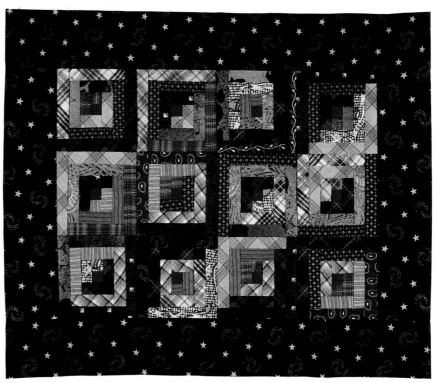

Mini Log Cabin by Lesly-Claire Greenberg, 1987, Fairfax, Virginia, 11⅜" x 14".

CUTTING

Cut ⅞"-wide strips and then logs, following the chart below.

Fabric	Number of Strips	Log Number	Log Length	Number of Logs
light or dark	1	Center	⅞"	12
light	1	1	⅞"	12
light	1	2	1⅛"	12
dark	1	3	1⅛"	12
dark	1	4	1⅝"	12
light	1	5	1⅝"	12
light	1	6	2"	12
dark	1	7	2"	12
dark	1	8	2¼"	12
light	1	9	2¼"	12
light	1	10	2¾"	12
dark	1	11	2¾"	12
dark	1	12	3⅛"	12

DIRECTIONS

If you have not made a sample block before starting this quilt, make one now, referring to Sewing on the Line, beginning on page 18.

Log Cabin Piecing

Make 12 Log Cabin blocks, following the piecing directions below.

1. Place the center square, right side up, on the unmarked side of the foundation. Hold the foundation up to the light and make sure the center square covers the area marked C.
2. Place log #1 on top of the center square, with right sides together. Hold the foundation up to the light and make sure log #1 and the center square cover the area marked C and extend the width of a seam allowance on all sides.
3. Turn the foundation over while carefully holding the logs in place; sew on the line between C and log #1.
4. Finger press log #1 open. Pin, if necessary, to keep log open and flat.
5. Add log #2 in the same way. Sew on the line between log #2 and log #1/C. Finger press log #2 and pin, if necessary, to keep log open and flat.
6. Continue adding logs in numerical order until the design is completed. Remember: logs #1 and #2 are light; logs #3 and #4 are dark; logs #5 and #6 are light; logs #7 and #8 dark, and so on.
7. Press completed block and trim to square up edges, leaving a ¼"-wide seam allowance beyond the outer line of the marked square.

Quilt Top Assembly

1. Arrange blocks into 3 rows of 4 blocks each, as shown in the photo on page 32, or create your own design. Pin the blocks together, matching the outer lines of the marked squares and sew on the line. Press the seams of alternate rows in opposite directions.
2. Join rows, making sure to match the seams between each block.
3. Cut 2 border strips, each 2¼" x 8⅜", and sew to the sides of the quilt top. Cut 2 border strips, each 2¼" x 14½", and sew to the top and bottom edges of the quilt top.

Finishing

1. Cut backing and batting the same size as the quilt top. Place batting on the wrong side of the quilt top, then place the quilt top on backing, right sides together. Sew around the edges, leaving an opening on one side for turning. Clip corners and turn right side out.
2. Blindstitch the opening closed; quilt.

***Note:** You may finish the quilt in the traditional manner if you prefer. Layer the quilt top with batting and backing and quilt as desired. Finish the edges with binding.*

OVER UNDER

Quilt Size: 18" x 18"

Finished Block: 3"

Use 3" Rail Fence block template on page 67 and 3" Quarter-Square Log Cabin block template on page 68.

1
2
3
4

Rail Fence

Quarter-Square

Over Under by Lesly-Claire Greenberg, 1992, Fairfax, Virginia, 18" x 18". This quilt was pieced on paper foundations.

MATERIALS
44"-wide fabric

16 Quarter-Square Log Cabin foundations
20 Rail Fence foundations

Fabric for Quarter-Square Log Cabin Blocks
Fabric a (bright) ⅛ yd.
Fabric b (light) ⅛ yd.
Fabric c (medium) ⅛ yd.
Fabric d (dark) ⅛ yd.

Fabric for Light Rail Blocks
Fabric A (lightest) ⅛ yd.
Fabric B (light) ⅛ yd.
Fabric C (light) ⅛ yd.
Fabric D (medium-light)⅛

Fabric for Dark Rail Blocks
Fabric E (medium) ⅛ yd.
Fabric F (medium-dark) ⅛ yd.
Fabric G (dark) ⅛ yd.
Fabric H (darkest) ⅛ yd.

Backing
⅝ yd.

Note: *You can also use one of the packs of hand-dyed fabrics, featuring 8 color gradations, which are available in many quilt shops.*

CUTTING

Cut all strips across the fabric width (crosswise grain).

Quarter-Square Log Cabin Blocks
Cut 1¼"-wide strips and then logs, following the chart below.

Fabric	Number of Strips	Log Number	Log Length	Number of Logs
a	1	1	1¼"	16
b	2	2	1¼"	16
		3	2"	16
c	2	4	2"	16
		5	2¾"	16
d	3	6	2¾"	16
		7	3½"	16

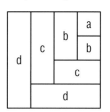

Color Pacement for
Quarter-Square Log Cabin Blocks

Make 16

Light Rail Fence Blocks
Cut 1¼"-wide strips and then logs, following the chart below.

Fabric	Number of Strips	Log Number	Log Length	Number of Logs
A	1	1	3½"	8
B	1	2	3½"	8
C	1	3	3½"	8
D	1	4	3½"	8

Color placement for
Light Rail Fence Blocks

A
B
C
D

Make 8

Dark Rail Fence Blocks
Cut 1¼"-wide strips and then logs, following the chart below.

Fabric	Number of Strips	Log Number	Log Length	Number of Logs
E	2	1	3½"	12
F	2	2	3½"	12
G	2	3	3½"	12
H	2	4	3½"	12

Color placement for
Dark Rail Fence Blocks

E
F
G
H

Make 12

DIRECTIONS

If you have not made a sample block before starting this quilt, make one now, referring to Sewing on the Line, beginning on page 18.

Quarter-Square Log Cabin Piecing

Make 16 Quarter-Square Log Cabin blocks, following the piecing directions below.

1. Place log #1, right side up, on the unmarked side of the foundation. Hold the foundation up to the light and make sure log #1 covers the area marked #1.
2. Place log #2 on top of log #1, with right sides together. Hold the foundation up to the light and make sure that log #1 and log #2 cover the area marked #1 and extend the width of a seam allowance on all sides.
3. Turn the foundation over while carefully holding the logs in place and sew on the line between log #1 and log #2.
4. Finger press log #2 open. Pin, if necessary, to keep log open and flat.
5. Continue to add logs in numerical order. Press completed block and trim to square up edges, leaving ¼"-wide seam allowances beyond the outer line of the marked square.

Rail Fence Piecing

Following the piecing directions below, make 20 Rail Fence blocks: 8 Light Rail Fence blocks (fabrics A, B, C, and D), and 12 Dark Rail Fence blocks (fabrics E, F, G, and H).

1. Place log #1, right side up, on the unmarked side of the foundation. Hold the foundation up to the light and make sure log #1 covers the area marked #1.
2. Place log #2 on top of log #1, with right sides together. Hold the foundation up to the light and make sure that log #1 and log #2 cover the area marked #1 and extend the width of a seam allowance on all sides.
3. Turn the foundation over while carefully holding the logs in place and sew on the line between log #1 and log #2.
4. Finger press log #2 open. Pin, if necessary, to keep log open and flat.
5. Complete the block by adding logs #3 and #4 in the same manner. Press completed block and trim to square up edges, leaving a ¼"-wide seam allowance beyond the outer line of the marked square.

Quilt Top Assembly

1. Paying careful attention to the orientation of each block, arrange blocks as shown to make 4 Ninepatch blocks. Each Ninepatch block requires 4 Quarter-Square Log Cabin blocks and 5 Rail Fence blocks (2 light and 3 dark).

2. Pin blocks into 3 rows of 3 blocks each, matching the outer lines of the marked squares, and sew on the line. Press the seams of alternate rows in opposite directions.

3. Join rows together to complete the Ninepatch blocks, making sure to match the seams between each block.

4. Arrange completed Ninepatch blocks as shown at right, rotating each square clockwise ¼ turn. Sew blocks together to complete the quilt top, making sure to match the seams between the blocks.

Finishing

1. Add borders as desired.
2. Cut backing and batting the same size as the quilt top.
3. To finish with the stitch-and-turn method, place batting on the wrong side of the quilt top, then place quilt top on backing, with right sides together. Sew around the edges, leaving an opening on one side for turning. Clip corners and turn right side out.
4. Blindstitch the opening closed; quilt.

Note: *You may finish the quilt in the traditional manner if you prefer. Layer the quilt top with batting and backing and quilt as desired. Finish the edges with binding.*

COLLECTOR'S VEST

This vest is a wonderful showcase for your pin or button collection. A full-size pattern in four sizes is given on the pullout pattern insert. Trace the pieces, following the cutting lines for your size. Choose from Small (30–32), Medium (34–36), Large (38–40), or Extra Large (42–44). Read the directions for making the vest before beginning.

Use 2½" Collector's Square block template on page 68.

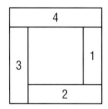

Collector's Square

Collector's Vests by Lesly-Claire Greenberg, 1986, Fairfax, Virginia.

MATERIALS
44"-wide fabric

Collector's Square foundations*

Center
Small: ¼ yd.
All other sizes: ⅓ yd.

Assorted Lights
(logs #1 and #2)
Small: ¼ yd.
All other sizes: ⅓ yd.

Assorted Darks
(logs #3 and #4)
Small: ⅓ yd.
All other sizes: ½ yd.

Back Interfacing (muslin)
Small, Medium: ⅝ yd.
Large, Extra Large: ¾ yd.
(to add equal weight to back)

Vest Back
Fabric of your choice
Small, Medium: ⅝ yd.
Large, Extra Large: ¾ yd.

Lining
Small, Medium: ⅝ yd.
Large, Extra Large: 1 yd.

*I recommend using cloth foundations for weight and stability.

CUTTING

Cut all strips across the fabric width (crosswise grain).

For the centers, cut 2"-wide strips and then cut into 2" x 2" squares, following the chart below.

	S	M	L	XL		S	M	L	XL
Center	4	5	5	5	Center 2" x 2"	72	84	86	90

Cut 1"-wide strips and then logs, following the chart below.

Fabric	Number of Strips				Log Number	Log Length	Number of Logs			
	S	M	L	XL			S	M	L	XL
light #1	4	5	5	5	1	2"	72	84	86	90
light #2	5	6	6	6	2	2½"	72	84	86	90
dark #1	5	6	6	6	3	2½"	72	84	86	90
dark #2	6	7	7	7	4	3"	72	84	86	90

DIRECTIONS

If you have not made a sample block before starting this vest, make one now, referring to Sewing on the Line, beginning on page 18.

Collector's Square Piecing

Make the number of Collector's Square blocks required for the size vest you are making, following the block piecing directions below.

1. Place the center square, right side up, on the unmarked side of the foundation. Hold the foundation up to the light and make sure the square covers the center area and extends the width of a seam allowance on all sides.

2. Place log #1 on top of the center square, with right sides together. Hold the foundation up to the light and make sure that log #1 extends the width of a seam allowance into the areas marked #1, #2, and #4.

3. Turn the foundation over while carefully holding the logs in place; sew on the line between the center and log #1.

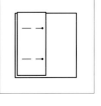
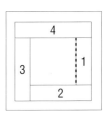

4. Finger press the log open over the area marked #1. Pin, if necessary, to keep log open and flat.

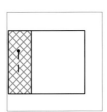

Opening log #1

5. Place log #2 on top of the center square, with right sides together. Hold the foundation up to the light and make sure that log #2 extends the width of a seam allowance into the areas marked #2, #1, and #3. Sew on the line between #2 and #1/center.

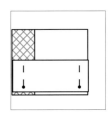

Place log #2

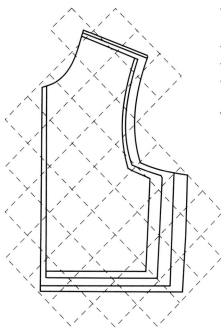

6. Finger press the log open over the area marked #2. Pin, if necessary, to keep log open and flat.
7. Add logs #3 and #4 in the same manner.
8. Press completed blocks and trim to square up the edges, leaving a ¼"-wide seam allowance beyond the outer line of the marked square.

Vest

Trace the pattern pieces on the pullout pattern insert onto tissue paper or pattern tracing cloth. Reverse the pattern for the right vest front. Transfer the circles on the vest front pattern to your paper pattern.

Vest Front Block Layout

1. Arrange the blocks on the left vest front, following the block placement guide on the vest front pattern piece. Reverse placement of blocks for right front. To create light and dark vertical stripes as shown in the sample vest, place blocks on the diagonal and alternate the direction of the light side of the blocks as indicated by the letters A (light) and B (dark) in the corners of each block.
2. Pin blocks together in diagonal rows, matching the outer lines on the marked squares, and sew on the line. Press seams of alternate rows in opposite directions.
3. Join the rows, making sure to match the seams between each block. Press seams open.
4. Using a pencil or other marking tool, transfer the circles from the paper pattern onto the pieced blocks.

Vest Construction

Use ¼"-wide seam allowances for assembling vest.
1. Place left front pattern on pieced blocks assembled for the left front. Match the circles on the pieced blocks with the circles on the pattern. Cut out the left front.
2. Place right front pattern on pieced fabric assembled for the right front. Match the circles on the pieced blocks with the circles on the pattern. Use the cutout left front to line up the blocks on the left and right sides. Cut out right front.
3. Cut 1 vest back from the muslin and 1 vest back from the chosen fabric. Sew the muslin to the wrong side of the vest back, stitching ³⁄₁₆" from the raw edges at neckline and side seams.

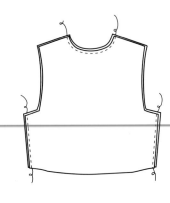

With right sides together, sew vest front to vest back at the shoulder seams.

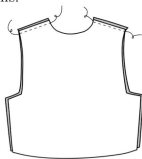

4. Cut 1 vest back, 1 left front, and 1 right front from the lining. With right sides together, sew the vest back lining to left and right vest front lining at the shoulder seams. Press seams open.

5. With right sides together, pin the lining to the vest, matching shoulder seams and having all raw edges even. Stitch lining to vest, leaving side seams open for turning. Clip curves, corners, and pivot points at square armhole.

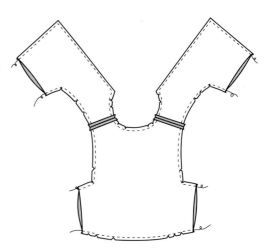

6. Turn vest right side out by pulling each front through the shoulder and out one of the back side openings as shown. Press carefully.

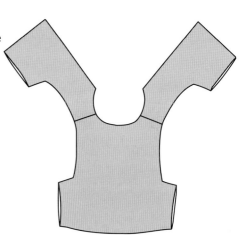

7. With right sides together and raw edges even, pin vest front to back at sides, matching armhole and lower edge seams. Starting on the lining 1" above the armhole seam, stitch vest side seams, ending stitching on lining 1" below seam at bottom edge of vest as shown.

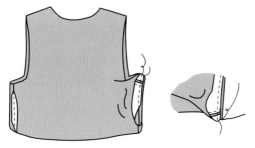

8. Press side seams toward vest back. Turn under side seam allowances on lining back and blindstitch to lining on front side seam allowance.

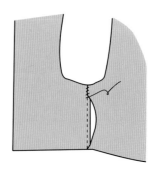

9. Embellish the block centers with your favorite buttons or pins.

PINEAPPLE

Quilt Size: 7" x 9½"

Finished Block: 2½"

Use 2½" Pineapple block template on page 69.

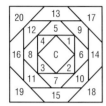

Pineapple

MATERIALS
44"-wide fabric

6 Pineapple foundations

Assorted scraps of light and dark fabrics

Border ¼ yd.
Backing ¼ yd.

Miniature Pineapple by Judy Spahn, 1987, Fairfax, Virginia, 7" x 9½".

CUTTING

For the center logs, cut 6 squares, each 1" x 1", from a light or a dark fabric. From assorted light and dark fabric scraps, cut ⅞"-wide strips for logs #1 through #16 and then crosscut into logs, following the chart below.

Fabric	Number of Strips	Log Number	Log Length	Number of Logs
dark	1	1	1"	6
dark	1	2	1"	6
dark	1	3	1"	6
dark	1	4	1"	6
light	1	5	1½"	6
light	1	6	1½"	6
light	1	7	1½"	6
light	1	8	1½"	6
dark	1	9	1½"	6
dark	1	10	1½"	6
dark	1	11	1½"	6
dark	1	12	1½"	6
light	1	13	2"	6
light	1	14	2"	6
light	1	15	2"	6
light	1	16	2"	6

From assorted dark fabric scraps, cut 1½"-wide strips for logs #17 through #20 (corners) and then crosscut into 2" log lenths.

Fabric	Number of Strips	Log Number	Log Length	Number of Logs
dark	1	17	2"	6
dark	1	18	2"	6
dark	1	19	2"	6
dark	1	20	2"	6

DIRECTIONS

If you have not made a sample block before starting this quilt, make one now, referring to Sewing on the Line, beginning on page 18.

Pineapple Piecing

Make 6 Pineapple blocks, following the piecing directions below.

1. Place the center square, right side up, on the unmarked side of the foundation. Hold the foundation up to the light and make sure the center square covers the area marked C and extends the width of a seam allowance on all sides.

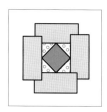

2. Place log #1 (dark) on top of the center square, with right sides together. Hold the foundation up to the light and make sure that log #1 and the center square cover the area marked C and extend the width of a seam allowance into adjacent areas.

3. Turn the foundation over while carefully holding the logs in place; sew on the line between C and log #1.

4. Finger press log #1 open. Pin, if necessary, to keep the log open and flat.

5. Sew logs #2, #3, and #4 (darks) in the same manner. Be sure to sew on the lines.

6. After sewing round 1, trim corners of logs #1, #2, #3, and #4 so that they extend only the width of a seam allowance into adjacent areas. See rule #3 on page 19.

7. Finger press each piece open and pin, if necessary, to keep it open and flat.

8. Continue adding logs in numerical order, using the appropriate light or dark fabrics. Each round of logs will be added at a 45° angle to the previous round of logs. Remember to sew on the line and trim for placement after sewing each round.

9. Press completed block and trim to square up edges, leaving a ¼"-wide seam allowance beyond the outer line of the marked square.

Quilt Top Assembly

1. Arrange blocks into 2 rows of 3 blocks each as shown in the photo on page 42. Pin blocks together, matching the outer lines of the marked squares and sew on the line. Press the seams of alternate rows in opposite directions.

2. Join rows, making sure to match the seams between each block. Press seams open.

3. Cut 4 strips, each 1½" wide, for borders. Sew borders to each side and then to the top and bottom edges of the quilt top. Apply borders with your choice of the straight-cut or mitered-corner methods.

Finishing

1. Cut backing and batting the same size as the quilt top.

2. To finish with the stitch-and-turn method, place batting on the wrong side of the quilt top, then place quilt top on backing, with right sides together. Sew around the edges, leaving an opening on one side for turning. Clip corners and turn right side out.

3. Blindstitch the opening closed; quilt.

Note: *You may finish the quilt in the traditional manner if you prefer. Layer the quilt top with batting and backing and quilt as desired. Finish the edges with binding.*

SQUARE IN A SQUARE VARIATION

Square in a Square Variation by Barb Celio, 1992, Vienna, Virginia, 17½" x 17½".

Quilt Size: 17½" x 17½"

Finished Block: 3"

Use 3" Virginia Reel block template on page 68.

Compare this quilt to the Virginia Reel quilt on page 48. Notice how color placement can cause a dramatic change in a quilt pattern.

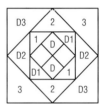

Virginia Reel

MATERIALS
44"-wide fabric

16 Virginia Reel Foundations

Light ⅛ yd. (center)
Light ⅛ yd. (1)
Medium ⅛ yd. (2)
Medium ⅛ yd. (D2)
Bright ¼ yd. (3 and D3)
Dark ⅛ yd. (center)
Dark ⅛ yd. (D1)
Dark ¼ yd. (3 and D3)

Inner border ⅛ yd.
Middle border ⅛ yd.
Outer border ¼ yd.
Backing ½ yd.

CUTTING

Cut all strips across the fabric width (crosswise grain).

Cut strips and then logs, following the chart below.

Fabric	Strip Width	Number of Strips	Log Number	Log Length	Number of Logs
Light (center)	1"	2	center	3"	16
Light	1"	2	1	1½"	32
Medium	1¼"	2	2	2"	32
Medium	1¼"	2	D2	2"	32
Bright	1¾"	3	3 & D3	2¾"	32
Dark (center)	1"	2	center	3"	16
Dark	1"	2	D1	1½"	32
Dark	1¾"	3	3 & D3	2¾"	32

DIRECTIONS

If you have not made a sample block before starting this quilt, make one now, referring to Sewing on the Line, beginning on page 18.

Virginia Reel Piecing

The center square and the first and second sets of logs are the same in each of the blocks. Eight blocks have dark outer triangles and eight blocks have bright outer triangles. To make this easy, first piece all 16 blocks, following steps 1–8. Then complete the blocks in 2 sets of 8, following steps 9 and 10.

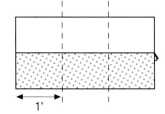
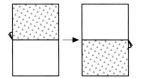

1. Piece the center Four Patch block. Sew a 3" dark log to a 3" light log, with right sides together. Press seam toward the dark fabric. Cut 2 units, each 1" wide. (There will be some waste.)

2. Join the units as shown to make a Four Patch block, matching the center seams.

3. Place a Four Patch square, right side up, on the unmarked side of the foundation, aligning the seam lines of the square to the lines on the foundation. Hold the foundation up to the light and make sure the Four Patch covers the center area and extends the width of a seam allowance into the adjacent areas.

4. Place log #1 on one side of the center square, with right sides together. Turn the foundation over while carefully holding logs in place; sew on the line between the center square and log #1. Sew second log #1 to opposite side of square.

5. Press logs open. Pin, if necessary, to keep logs open and flat.

Logs #1 and #D1 added to center Four Patch

6. Place log #D1 on top of the center square and log #1. Turn the foundation over while holding the logs in place and sew on the line between the center square and log #D1. Sew second log #D1 to opposite side of square.

7. Trim excess fabric on logs to make placing the next logs easier. Fold the foundation back and trim the corner of the

logs at a 45°angle so that a ¼"-wide seam allowance extends into the adjacent areas. See rule #3, page 19. Press logs open and pin to keep logs open and flat.

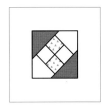

Trim corners of logs #1 and #D1.

8. Add logs #2 and #D2 to all 16 blocks.
9. Divide the 16 blocks into 2 sets. Complete 8 blocks, using the bright fabric for logs #3 and #D3. Complete the remaining 8 blocks, using a dark fabric for logs #3 and #D3.
10. Press completed blocks and trim to square up edges, leaving a ¼"-wide seam allowance beyond the outer line of the marked square.

Quilt Top Assembly

1. Arrange blocks as shown in the photo on page 45. Alternate the bright and dark blocks, rotating the blocks as shown. Pin blocks in 4 rows of 4 blocks each, matching the outer lines of the marked squares, and sew on the line. Press the seams of alternate rows in opposite directions.
2. Join rows, making sure to match the seams between each block. Press seams open.
3. For the inner borders, cut 2 strips, each 1" x 12½", and 2 strips, each 1" x 13½". Sew the 12½"-long strips to opposite sides, and the 13½"-long strips to the other 2 sides of the quilt top.
4. Cut 2 strips, each ¾" x 13½", and 2 strips, each ¾" x 14", for the middle borders. Sew the 13½"-long strips to opposite sides of the quilt top, and the 14"-long strips to the other 2 sides of the quilt top.
5. For the outer borders, cut 2 strips, each 2½" x 14", and 2 strips, each 2½" x 18". Sew the 14"-long strips to opposite sides of the quilt top, and the 18"-long strips to the other 2 sides of the quilt top.

Finishing

1. Cut backing and batting the same size as the quilt top.
2. To finish with the stitch-and-turn method, place batting on the wrong side of the quilt top, then place quilt top on backing, with right sides together. Sew around the edges, leaving an opening on one side for turning. Clip corners and turn right side out.
3. Blindstitch the opening closed; quilt as desired.

Note: *You may finish the quilt in the traditional manner if you prefer. Layer the quilt top with batting and backing and quilt as desired. Finish the edges with binding.*

VIRGINIA REEL

Quilt Size: 17" x 23"

Finished Block: 3"

Use 3" Virginia Reel block template on page 68.

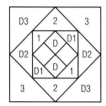

Virginia Reel

MATERIALS
44"-wide fabric

24 Virginia Reel foundations

Dark ½ yd.
Light ½ yd.

Border ⅓ yd.
Backing ¾ yd.

Note: *The yardage given above is for a quilt made in two colors only, one light and one dark. If you prefer a scrappy quilt, use an assortment of light and dark scraps. Fabric scraps should be at least 3½" x 9" in order to cut the required number of logs for one-half of a block (either light or dark).*

Virginia Reel by Lesly-Claire Greenberg, 1990, Fairfax, Virginia, 17" x 23". Additional blocks pieced by Kaye Rhodes and Mary Ann Rush.

Cut all strips across the fabric width (crosswise grain).

CUTTING FOR A TWO-COLOR QUILT					
Fabric	Number of Strips	Strip Width	Log Number	Log Length	Number of Logs
Dark	2	1"	D	3"	24
	2	1"	D1	1½"	48
	3	1¼"	D2	2"	48
	4	1¾"	D3	2¾"	48
Light	2	1"	center	3"	24
	2	1"	1	1½"	48
	3	1¼"	2	2"	48
	4	1¾"	3	2¾"	48

CUTTING FOR ONE BLOCK IN A SCRAP QUILT*				
Fabric	Strip Width	Log Number	Log Length	Number of Logs
Dark	1"	D	3"	1
	1"	D1	1½"	2
	1¼"	D2	2"	2
	1¾"	D3	2¾"	2
Light	1"	center	3"	1
	1"	1	1½"	2
	1¼"	2	2"	2
	1¾"	3	2¾"	2

*You will need to repeat this for 24 blocks.

DIRECTIONS

If you have not made a sample block before starting this quilt, make one now, referring to Sewing on the Line, beginning on page 18.

Virginia Reel Piecing

Make 24 Virginia Reel blocks, following the piecing directions below.

1. Sew log D (3" dark) to a 3" light log (center), with right sides together. Press seam toward the dark fabric. Cut 2 units, each 1" wide. (There will be some waste.)

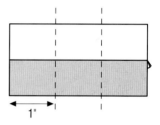

2. Join the 1" units as shown to make 1 Four Patch block, matching the center seams.

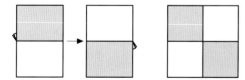

3. Place a Four Patch square, right side up, on the unmarked side of the foundation, aligning the seams of the square to the lines on the foundation. Hold the foundation up to a light and make sure the Four Patch covers the center area and extends the width of a seam allowance into the adjacent areas. Be sure the dark patch aligns with "D."

4. Place log #1 on one side of the center square, with right sides together. Hold the foundation up to the light and make sure that log #1 extends the width of a seam allowance into the adjacent areas.

5. Turn the foundation over while carefully holding logs in place; sew on the line between the center square and #1. Sew the second log #1 to the opposite side of the square.

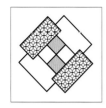

Logs #1 and #D1 added to
center Four Patch

Trim corners of logs #1 and #D1.

6. Press logs open. Pin, if necessary, to hold logs open and flat.
7. Place log #D1 on top of the center square and log #1. Turn the foundation over while holding the logs in place; sew on the line between the center square and log #D1. Sew the second log #D1 to the opposite side of the square.

8. Trim excess fabric to make placing the next logs easier. Fold the foundation back and trim the corner of the logs at an angle so that a ¼"-wide seam allowance extends into the adjacent areas. See rule #3, page 19. Press logs open and pin to keep logs open and flat.

9. Continue adding logs in numerical order, paying careful attention to the placement of light and dark logs. Remember to trim after each round to make placing the next logs easier.
10. Press completed block and trim to square up edges, leaving a ¼"-wide seam allowance beyond the outer line of the marked square.

Quilt Top Assembly
1. Arrange the blocks in 6 rows of 4 blocks each, as shown in the photo on page 48. To achieve the reel pattern, rotate the blocks so that 4 light corners or 4 dark corners meet. Pin the blocks together, matching the outer lines of the marked squares, and sew on the line. Press the seams of alternate rows in opposite directions.
2. Join rows, making sure to match the seams between each block. Press seams open.
3. For borders, cut 2 strips, each 3" x 18½", and 2 strips, each 3" x 17½". Sew the 18½"-long strips to the long sides of the quilt top, and the 17½"-long strips to the short sides of the quilt top.

Finishing
1. Cut backing and batting the same size as the quilt top.
2. To finish with the stitch-and-turn method, place batting on the wrong side of the quilt top, then place quilt top on backing, with right sides together. Sew around the edges, leaving an opening on one side for turning. Clip corners and turn right side out.
3. Blindstitch the opening closed; quilt as desired.

Note: *You may finish the quilt in the traditional manner if you prefer. Layer the quilt top with batting and backing and quilt as desired. Finish the edges with binding.*

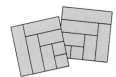

QUARTER-SQUARE LOG CABIN

Quarter-Square Log Cabin by Barb Celio, 1992, Vienna, Virginia, 31½" x 31½". The block was designed to allow the quilter to make quilts in larger sizes by "sewing on the line."

CUTTING

Cut all strips across the fabric width (crosswise grain).

For the center logs, cut 64 squares, each 1¼" x 1¼", from black. From each of the 4 color families, cut 1¼"-wide strips and then logs, following the chart below.

CUTTING CHART FOR EACH COLOR FAMILY				
Fabric	**Number of Strips**	**Log Number**	**Log Length**	**Number of Logs**
Light	2	2	1¼"	8
		3	2"	8
		6	2¾"	8
		7	3½"	8
Medium	2	4	2"	16
		5	2¾"	16
Dark	2	2	1¼"	8
		3	2"	8
		6	2¾"	8
		7	3½"	8

Note: *Lay out all blocks for placement before sewing. Some blocks will be made with all one color family, some will be made with two color families.*

Quilt Size: 31½" x 31½"

Finished Block: 3"

Use 3" Quarter-Square Log Cabin block template on page 68.

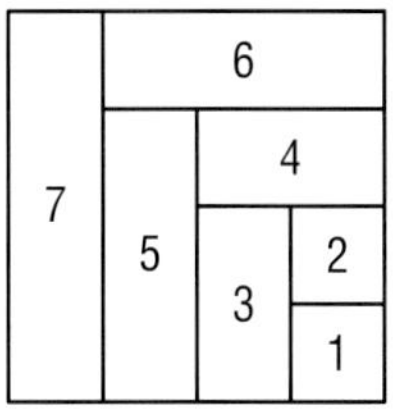

```
 ┌──────────────┐
 │      6       │
 │   ┌──────┬───┤
 │ 7 │    4 │   │
 │   │ 5 ┌──┴─┬─┤
 │   │   │  3 │2│
 │   │   │    ├─┤
 │   │   │    │1│
 └───┴───┴────┴─┘
```

Quarter-Square Log Cabin

MATERIALS
44"-wide fabric

64 Quarter-Square Log Cabin foundations

Center
Black ¼ yd.

Color Family 1
Light pink ⅛ yd.
Medium pink ⅛ yd.
Dark pink ⅛ yd.

Color Family 2
Light blue ⅛ yd.
Medium blue ⅛ yd.
Dark blue ⅛ yd.

Color Family 3
Lt. turquoise ⅛ yd.
Med. turquoise ⅛ yd.
Dark turquoise ⅛ yd.

Color Family 4
Light purple ⅛ yd.
Medium purple ⅛ yd.
Dark purple ⅛ yd.

Borders and Backing
Inner Border ¼ yd.
Middle Border ¼ yd.
Outer Border ¼ yd.
Backing 1 yd.

DIRECTIONS

If you have not made a sample block before starting this quilt, make one now, referring to Sewing on the Line, beginning on page 10.

Quarter-Square Log Cabin Piecing

This design calls for 8 different color variations of the 3" block, repeated 8 times each, for a total of 64 blocks.

Using appropriate fabrics from each color family, make blocks for color variations 1–4, following the diagram below for color placement. Make 8 of each variation.

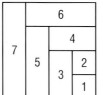

Make 8 from each color family.

Black 1
Dark 2 and 3
Medium 4 and 5
Light 6 and 7

Using appropriate fabrics from each color family, make blocks for color variations 5–8, following the diagram below for color placement. Make 8 of each variation.

Color Variation 5 - Make 8	Color Variation 6 - Make 8	Color Variation 7 - Make 8	Color Variation 8 - Make 8
Black 1	Black 1	Black 1	Black 1
Light pink 2	Light blue 2	Light turquoise 2	Light purple 2
Med. pink 4	Med. blue 4	Med. turquoise 4	Med. purple 4
Dark pink 6	Dark blue 6	Dark turquoise 6	Dark purple 6
Light blue 3	Light pink 3	Light purple 3	Light turquoise 3
Med. blue 5	Med. pink 5	Med. purple 5	Med. turquoise 5
Dark blue 7	Dark pink 7	Dark purple 7	Dark turquoise 7

1. Place log #1, right side up, on the unmarked side of the foundation. Hold the foundation up to the light and make sure that log #1 covers the area marked #1 and extends the width of a seam allowance into the adjacent areas.
2. Place log #2 on top of log #1, with right sides together. Hold the foundation up to the light and make sure that log #2 and log #1 cover the area marked #1, and extend the width of a seam allowance into the adjacent areas.
3. Turn the foundation over while carefully holding the logs in place; sew on the line between log #1 and log #2.
4. Finger press log #2 open. Pin, if necessary, to keep log open and flat.
5. Continue adding logs in numerical order. Press completed block and trim to square up edges, leaving a ¼"-wide seam allowance beyond the outer line of the marked square.

Quilt Top Assembly

1. Arrange 4 Quarter-Square Log Cabin blocks to make Four Patch blocks as shown or create your own design.

Block Placement of Color Variations

2	6
5	1

8	3
4	7

Four Patch A   Four Patch B

Pin blocks in pairs, matching outer lines of marked squares on both blocks. Sew on the line. Press seams of each pair of blocks in opposite directions. Sew pairs of blocks together, making sure to match the seams between each block.

2. Arrange Four Patch blocks in 4 rows of 4 blocks each, rotating blocks as shown at right. Sew blocks together into rows, making sure to match the seams between each block. Press seams of alternate rows in opposite directions.

2	6	8	3	2	6	8	3
5	1	4	7	5	1	4	7
7	4	1	5	7	4	1	5
3	8	6	2	3	8	6	2
2	6	8	3	2	6	8	3
5	1	4	7	5	1	4	7
7	4	1	5	7	4	1	5
3	8	6	2	3	8	6	2

Placement of Four Patch blocks and orientation of color variations.

3. Join rows, making sure to match the seams between each block, and sew on the line.
4. From each of the 3 border fabrics, cut 4 strips, each 1¾" x 40". (Cut across the fabric width.)
5. Sew the inner border to opposite sides, then to the top and bottom edges of the quilt top. Add the middle and then the outer borders in the same manner.

Finishing

1. Cut backing and batting the same size as the quilt top.
2. To finish with the stitch-and-turn method, place batting on the wrong side of the quilt top, then place quilt top on backing, with right sides together. Sew around the edges, leaving an opening on one side for turning. Clip corners and turn right side out.
3. Blindstitch the opening closed; quilt as desired.

Note: *You may finish the quilt in the traditional manner if you prefer. Layer the quilt top with batting and backing and quilt as desired. Finish the edges with binding.*

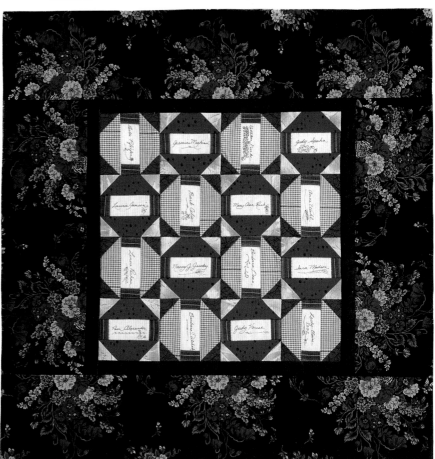

FRIENDSHIP STAR

Quilt Size: 19" x 19"

Finished Block: 3"

Use 3" Friendship Star block template on page 68.

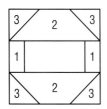

Friendship Star

MATERIALS
44"-wide fabric

16 Friendship Star foundations

White ⅛ yd.
Green ⅛ yd.
Red ⅛ yd.
Yellow ⅛ yd.
Dark red ⅛ yd.
Bright yellow ⅛ yd.

Inner border ⅛ yd.
Outer border ¼ yd.
Backing ⅝ yd.

Friendship Star by Lesly-Claire Greenberg, 1992, Fairfax, Virginia, 19" x 19". The star is formed in the corners of the squares when the color of the corners alternate light and dark. The center rectangle provides a space for signatures.

CUTTING

Cut all strips across the fabric width (crosswise grain).

Cut 1½"-wide strips and then logs, following the chart below.

Fabric	Number of Strips	Log Number	Log Length	Number of Logs
White	1	C	2½"	16
Green	1	1	1"	32
Red	2	2	3½"	16
Yellow	2	2	3½"	16
Dark red	2	3	2"	32
Bright yellow	2	3	2"	32

DIRECTIONS

If you have not made a sample block before starting this quilt, make one now, referring to Sewing on the Line, beginning on page 18.

Friendship Star Piecing

Make 16 Friendship Star blocks, following the piecing directions below. Make 8 blocks with red strips and yellow corners, and 8 blocks with yellow strips and red corners.

1. Place the center (signature strip), right side up, on the unmarked side of the foundation. Hold the foundation up to the light and make sure that the strip covers the center area and extends the width of a seam allowance on all sides.
2. Place log #1 (green) at one end of the center strip, with right sides together. Hold the foundation up to the light and make sure that log #1 extends the width of a seam allowance into the adjacent areas.

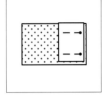

3. Turn the foundation over while carefully holding the logs in place; sew on the line between the center strip and log #1. Repeat steps 2 and 3 with second log #1 at the other end of the center strip.
4. Finger press both logs open. Pin, if necessary, to keep logs open and flat.
5. Place log #2 (red or yellow) on top of the center strip, with right sides together. Make sure log #2 extends the width of a seam allowance into the adjacent areas.

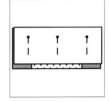

6. Turn the foundation over while holding the logs in place; sew on the line between log #2 and log #1/center strip. Repeat with second red (or yellow) log #2 on the other side.
7. Trim the corners of log #2 at an angle so that a ¼"-wide seam allowance extends into the area marked #3. (For help, refer to trimming of Pineapple Block Sample, page 19 and 24.) Finger press both logs open. Pin, if necessary, to keep logs open and flat.

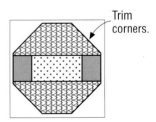

Trim corners.

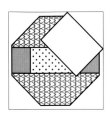

Align log #3 with edge of log #2.

8. Place log #3 (bright yellow or red) at one corner of log #2, with right sides together. You can align the long edge of log #3 with the trimmed edge of log #2.

Turn foundation over and stitch between logs #3 and #2. Finger press log #3 open over area marked 3. Repeat with log #3 in remaining corners.

9. Press completed block and trim to square up edges, leaving a ¼"-wide seam allowance beyond the outer line of each marked square.

Quilt Top Assembly

1. Arrange blocks as shown in the photo on page 54. Alternate the red and yellow blocks, placing the center signature strip vertically in the yellow blocks and horizontally in the red blocks. Pin blocks together in 4 rows of 4 blocks each, matching the outer lines of the marked squares, and sew on the line. Press the seams of alternate rows in opposite directions.

2. Join rows, making sure to match the seams between each block, and sew on the line.

3. For inner borders, cut 2 strips, each 1" x 12½", and 2 strips, each 1" x 13½". Sew the 12½"-long strips to opposite sides and the 13½"-long strips to the top and bottom edges of the quilt top. Remember to sew on the lines.

4. For outer borders, cut 2 strips, each 3½" x 13½", and 2 strips, each 3½" x 19½". Sew the 13½"-long strips to opposite sides and the 19½"-long strips to the top and bottom edges of the quilt top.

Finishing

1. Layer the quilt top with batting and backing; quilt as desired.

2. Bind the edges.

3. Signatures can be added when the quilt is completed, or at any stage of construction. You can use a decorative stamp with permanent fabric ink or decorate the signature strip with a permanent marking pen, such as Pigma™ or Pilot™ brand pens.

RECTANGLE TWIST

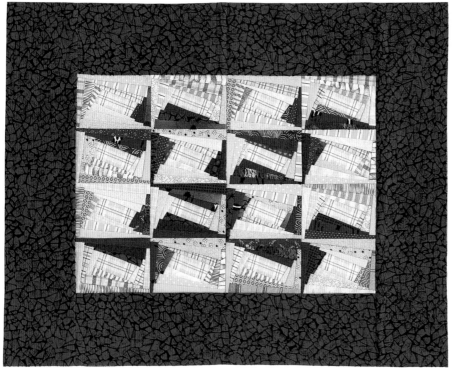

Rectangle Twist by Lesly-Claire Greenberg, 1993, Fairfax, Virginia, 22½" x 18". Dark and light sides of the blocks are alternated to form stars.

Quilt Size: 22½" x 18"

Finished Block: 4" x 2¾"

Use Rectangle Twist block template on page 70.

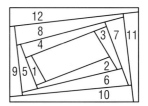

Rectangle Twist

MATERIALS
44"-wide fabric

16 Rectangle Twist foundations

Center ⅛ yd.

Scraps of 12 assorted yellows to total ¼ yd.

Scraps of 12 assorted blues to total ¼ yd.

Border ¼ yd.
Backing ⅝ yd.

CUTTING

The cutting chart on page 58 provides cutting information for using 12 different yellows and 12 different blues, and assumes that each fabric maintains the same position in each block. The blocks in the sample were chosen at random. When using totally random placement, only the strip width, log length, and number of logs need to be followed.

For the center log, cut 2 strips, each 1¼" wide, from yellow fabric, then crosscut the strips into 2¾" lengths to yield 16 center logs. Cut 1"-wide strips and then logs, following the chart on page 58.

Fabric	Number of Strips	Log Number	Log Length	Number of Logs
Blue 1 and Yellow 1	1	1	1¼"	8
Blue 2 and Yellow 2	1	2	3"	8
Blue 3 and Yellow 3	1	3	1¾"	8
Blue 4 and Yellow 4	1	4	3¼"	8
Blue 5 and Yellow 5	1	5	2"	8
Blue 6 and Yellow 6	1	6	3¾"	8
Blue 7 and Yellow 7	1	7	2½"	8
Blue 8 and Yellow 8	1	8	4"	8
Blue 9 and Yellow 9	1	9	2¾"	8
Blue 10 and Yellow 10	1	10	4½"	8
Blue 11 and Yellow 11	1	11	3¼"	8
Blue 12 and Yellow 12	1	12	4½"	8

Each block uses 6 logs in yellow and 6 logs in blue. Begin 8 blocks with log #1 yellow, and 8 blocks with log #1 blue. Alternate blue log, yellow log until all 12 logs are sewn.

DIRECTIONS

If you have not made a sample block before starting this quilt, make one now, referring to Sewing on the Line, beginning on page 18.

Rectangle Twist Piecing

Make 16 Rectangle Twist blocks, following the piecing directions below.

1. Place the center rectangle, right side up, on the unmarked side of the foundation. Hold the foundation up to the light and make sure the center rectangle covers the entire center area and extends the width of a seam allowance beyond all sides into the adjacent areas.
2. Place log #1 on top of the center rectangle, with right sides together. Hold the foundation up to the light and make sure that log #1 and the center extend on both ends into the adjacent areas.

3. Turn the foundation over while carefully holding the logs in place; sew on the line between the center and log #1.
4. Finger press log #1 open. Trim excess fabric, if necessary, to avoid bulk.
5. Add log #2 in the same way. Sew on the line between log #2 and log #1/center. Finger press log #2 and pin, if necessary, to keep log open and flat.
6. Continue adding logs in numerical order until the block is completed. (You will need to trim for placement after completing each round of 4 logs. Refer to rule #3 on page 19.) Remember: Logs #1, #3, #5, #7, #9, #11 (the short logs) are all one color, and logs #2, #4, #6, #8, #10, #12, (the long logs), are the other color.
7. Press completed block and trim to square up edges, leaving a ¼"-wide seam allowance beyond the outer line of the marked foundation.

Quilt Assembly

1. Arrange blocks into 4 rows of 4 blocks each, as shown in the photo on page 57, or create your own design. Pin the blocks together, matching the outer lines of the marked foundations and sew on the line. Press seams of alternate rows in opposite directions.
2. Join rows, making sure to match the seams between each block. Press seams open.
3. Cut strips for the borders 4" wide. Cut 2 strips, each 4" x 16", and 2 strips, each 4" x 18½". Sew 16" borders to long sides of the rectangle. Sew 18½" borders to remaining two sides.

Finishing

1. Cut backing and batting the same size as the quilt top.
2. To finish with the stitch-and-turn method, place batting on the wrong side of the quilt top, then place quilt top on backing, with right sides together. Sew around the edges, leaving an opening on one side for turning. Clip corners and turn right side out.
3. Blindstitch the opening closed; quilt.

Note: *You may finish the quilt in the traditional manner if you prefer. Layer the quilt top with batting and backing and quilt as desired. Finish the edges with binding.*

COURTHOUSE STEPS

Quilt Size: 8⅜" x 11"

Finished Block: 2⅝"

Use 2⅝" Courthouse Steps block template on page 69.

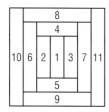

Courthouse Steps

MATERIALS
44"-wide fabric

12 Courthouse Step foundations

Center ⅛ yd.

Scraps at least 4" x 6" (Use 31 different prints to make each lantern a different color.)

Backing ⅓ yd.
Binding ¼ yd.

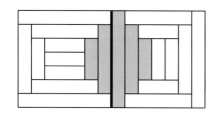

Night Light by Leslie Pfeifer, 1991, Fairfax, Virginia, 8⅜" x 11". This quilt was made with the leftover strips from Lesly-Claire's Flower Drum Song.

ADVANCE PLANNING

This quilt requires some advance planning. Once the fabrics have been selected, you must also pay particular attention to the placement of the fabrics when sewing the blocks. It is very important to follow the directions below to make a mock-up. It will be both your cutting and your sewing guide. See page 71 for instructions on making a fabric mock-up.

The Courthouse Steps block is made up of 11 logs—two logs each on two opposite sides of the center log, and three logs each on the other two sides. By alternating vertical blocks with horizontal blocks, the two-log side meets the three-log side of the next block. The lantern pattern is achieved by using the same fabric on the two-log side of one block and the three-log side of the adjacent block. The center strip remains the same in each block.

1. Using the Courthouse Steps grid on page 77 or a grid that you've created yourself, number each block as shown at right. Using a large grid will make it easier to color the logs or to glue strips of fabric in the correct position.

2. Begin in the top left corner with block 1A. Each block requires 4 different fabrics. Color the logs or glue 4 selected fabrics in place.

3. Move to the next block, 1B. Select 3 new fabrics plus the 1 adjacent fabric from the first block, 1A, for the fourth fabric in 1B. Color or glue fabrics in place.

4. Move to the next block, 1C. Select 3 new fabrics, and again select the 1 adjacent fabric from the previous block, 1B, as the fourth fabric.

Note: Some blocks require that you select only 2 new fabrics and the remaining 2 fabrics from adjacent blocks.

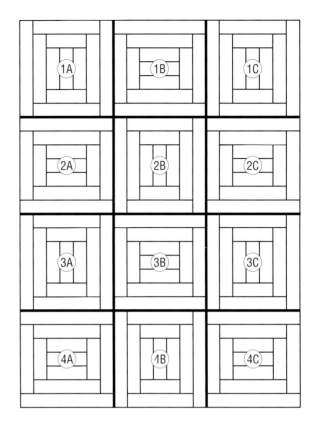

5. Continue to select fabrics for each block and complete your fabric or color mock-up in this manner, following the chart below. This may look like a time-consuming process, but the results are well worth it.

Note: To achieve the lantern pattern, the two-log side of one block must match the three-log side of the adjacent block.

Block Color Planning Guide

Block 1A — 4 different fabrics
Block 1B — 3 new fabrics, the 4th from 1A
Block 1C — 3 new fabrics, the 4th from 1B
Block 2A — 3 new fabrics, the 4th from 1A
Block 2B — 2 new fabrics, the 3rd from 1B, the 4th from 2A
Block 2C — 2 new fabrics, the 3rd from 1C, the 4th from 2B
Block 3A — 3 new fabrics, the 4th from 2A
Block 3B — 2 new fabrics, the 3rd from 2B, the 4th from 3A
Block 3C — 2 new fabrics, the 3rd from 2C, the 4th from 3B
Block 4A — 3 new fabrics, the 4th from 3A
Block 4B — 2 new fabrics, the 3rd from 3B, the 4th from 4A
Block 4C — 2 new fabrics, the 3rd from 3C, the 4th from 4B

CUTTING

Cutting instructions for this quilt are a little tricky because so many different fabrics are used and only a few logs need to be cut from each fabric. Only lanterns found on the interior of the quilt are made up of five logs (two from one block and three from the adjacent block). Partial lanterns, found on the edges of the quilt, are made up of only two or three logs, depending upon the position of the block.

Once you have prepared your mock-up, you will know exactly where each fabric is positioned and how many logs are required from each fabric. Cut all strips 1" wide.

Using fabric for center, cut 12 logs, each 1" x 1½", for log #1.

For each interior lantern, cut the following strips from the same fabric. Cut strips from 17 different fabrics to make 17 different interior lanterns. Position logs for each block, following your mock-up.

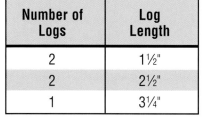

Number of Logs	Log Length
2	1½"
2	2½"
1	3¼"

Interior Lantern

For each three-sided edge lantern, cut the following strips from the same fabric. Cut strips from 7 different fabrics to make 7 different three-sided edge lanterns. Position logs for each block, following your mock-up.

Number of Logs	Log Length
1	1½"
1	2½"
1	3¼"

Three-sided Edge Lantern

For each two-sided edge lantern, cut the following strips from the same fabric. Cut strips from 7 different fabrics to make 7 different two-sided edge lanterns. Position logs for each block, following your mock-up.

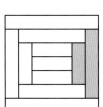

Number of Logs	Log Length
1	1½"
1	2½"

Two-sided Edge Lantern

DIRECTIONS

If you have not made a sample block before starting this quilt, make one now, referring to Sewing on the Line, beginning on page 18.

Courthouse Steps Piecing

Make 12 Courthouse Steps blocks, following the piecing directions below.

1. Place log #1, right side up, on the unmarked side of the foundation over the area marked #1.
2. Place log #2 on log #1, with right sides together. Hold the foundation up to the light and make sure the logs cover the area marked #1 and extend the width of a seam allowance into the adjacent areas.
3. Turn the foundation over while carefully holding the logs in place; sew on the line between #1 and #2.
4. Finger press log open. Pin, if necessary, to keep log open and flat.
5. Place log #3 on top of log #1, with right sides together. Hold the foundation up to the light and make sure log #3 extends the width of a seam allowance into the adjacent areas.
6. Turn the foundation over while carefully holding the logs in place and sew on the line between #1 and #3.
7. Finger press log open. Pin, if necessary, to keep log open and flat.
8. Continue adding logs in numerical order. Remember to follow your color mock-up so that the fabrics in one block match up with the fabrics in the adjacent blocks to create the lantern pattern.
9. Press completed blocks and trim to square up the edges, leaving a ¼"-wide seam allowance beyond the outer line of the marked square.

Quilt Top Assembly

1. Arrange the blocks according to your color mock-up. Pin blocks together in 3 rows of 4 blocks each, making sure to match the outer line of the marked square, and sew on the line. Press seams of alternate rows in opposite directions.
2. Join rows, making sure to match the seams between the blocks.

Finishing

1. Layer quilt top with batting and backing; quilt as desired.
2. Bind the edges.

The cover quilt (also shown on page 19) has 130 blocks. It contains over 100 different fabrics, but remember, you only need a small amount of each fabric.

If you'd like to make this stunning quilt, make a grid of Courthouse Steps blocks 10 blocks wide by 13 blocks long. Color or glue fabrics in place to create a color mock-up as described on page 61.

From your color mock-up, determine the number of interior lanterns, and two- and three-sided lanterns needed. Cut fabric for lanterns, following the cutting directions on page 62. Piece blocks and assemble quilt, following the directions for the wall hanging and joining blocks into 13 rows of 10 blocks each.

Any design that can be completed with basic strip piecing on a foundation—starting in one place and covering raw edges with the next pieces until the entire foundation is covered—can probably be done using my method of sewing on the line. Piecing can start any place on the unit—in the center, off center, or on an edge—as long as the next piece covers the raw edge of the previous piece. Antique crazy quilts were done in this manner. The difference is that the design is planned first so a foundation can be prepared with marked lines for sewing on the line.

The very first piece in which I used this technique was a Mariner's Compass design I did on a cape for the inaugural run of the Fairfield Fashion Show in 1980. The cape appears in Virginia Avery's book *Quilts to Wear*.

You can design blocks of any shape. Squares, of course, are the easiest. To start, draft the unit or overall design that you wish to piece. Divide the design into the largest possible units that you can use to attain your design. Analyze the construction of each unit. Adapt the unit design so that the foundation can be covered. Plan the project, using color sketches if necessary, and dive in.

When designing your original project for sewing on the line, be sure to give yourself as much creative room as possible. Investigate different block sizes, or try combining several different blocks in one project. Try compressing units into different shapes or distorting them by stretching them out.

Here are some ideas for simple variations to get you started in the creative direction, using the block designs given in this book. See page 71 for Using Design Grids.

SAME BLOCK—DIFFERENT COLORS

Color the block in two or more ways and combine the blocks, forming an overall color design.

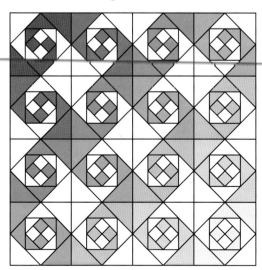

SAME BLOCK—BLOCK ROTATION

Using a design grid, place color to form a design different from the placement shown, or make the blocks and play with the placement until you are pleased with the layout.

Warning: This may be habit-forming; you run the risk of finding too many good designs and you won't remember half of them. Keep pencil and paper or a Polaroid camera handy to record the good ones. See "A Touch of Yellow" on page 7 for an example of block rotation.

SAME BLOCK—DIFFERENT SIZE

Plan a design, using blocks made in different multiples of a size, for example, 2", 4", 8", etc. Using multiples makes it easy to plan units that can be easily pieced together so you don't have unusually shaped holes to fill in your design.

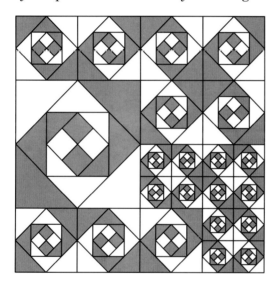

DIFFERENT BLOCKS—SAME SIZE

Combine two or more different block designs to add interest in one composition. Try blocks of different designs but the same size. Make them in the same or a similar color as a unifying factor. You can also base your design on units that all have the same-size strips for continuity. Varying the log widths might make the project more interesting.

DIFFERENT BLOCK—SAME SIZE— DIFFERENT COLOR

Use blocks made in several different color schemes. For example, all Log Cabin blocks could be in one color family and Pineapple blocks in a second color family. Varying the block placements in the layout creates different effects. Transparency and floating effects provide a third dimension. For the most contrast, use colors that are opposite each other on the color wheel. See "Over Under" in the project section, page 34.

DIFFERENT BLOCK—SAME SIZE— COLOR GRADATIONS

Use color to meld the blocks together. Try shading or gradations of color. Packets of hand-dyed fabrics in soft color gradations are perfect for creating this effect and give a floating, ethereal quality to a finished piece. This is what I tried to accomplish in "Interweave Too" (color photo on page 17), an Over Under color variation.

DIFFERENT SIZE BLOCK— DIFFERENT COLOR

Use different-size blocks and contrasting colors to form an alternate design or two designs that can be superimposed on each other. Experiment with the same contrasts that you used with the same-size blocks. This is the premise behind Ruth McDowell's book *Pattern on Pattern*.

BLOCK TEMPLATES

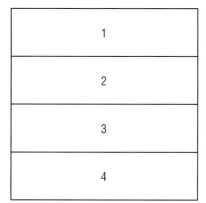

2" Rail Fence

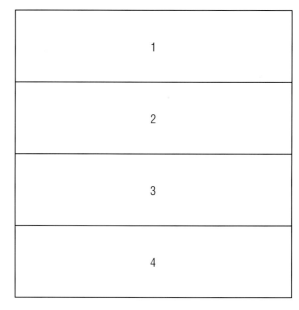

3" Rail Fence

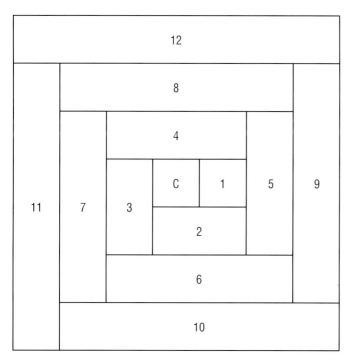

3½" Log Cabin

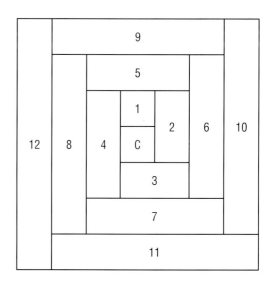

2⅝" Log Cabin

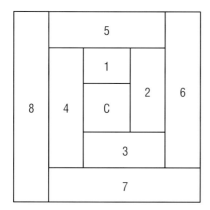

2" Log Cabin

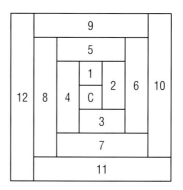

1¾" Log Cabin

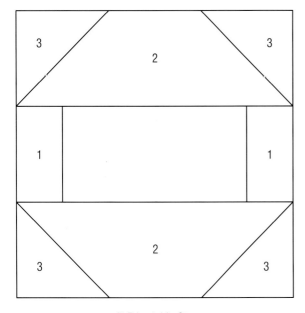

3" Friendship Star

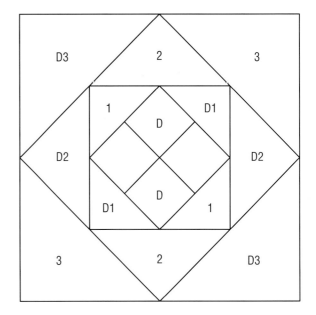

3" Virginia Reel

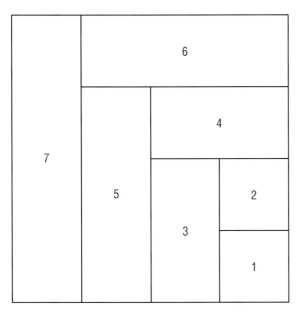

3" Quarter-Square Log Cabin

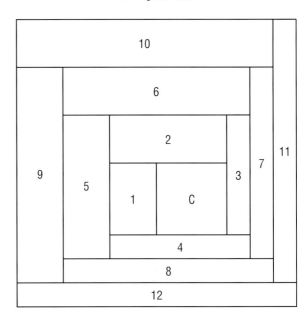

3" Offset Log Cabin

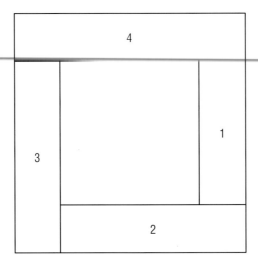

2½" Collector's Square

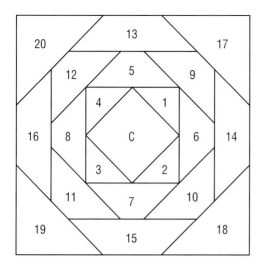

2½" Pineapple

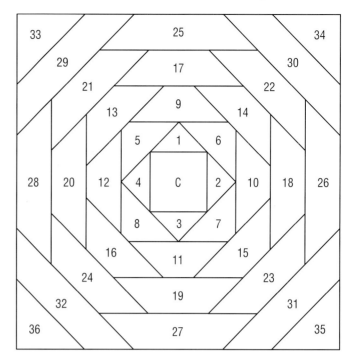

3½" Pineapple

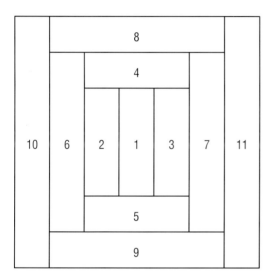

2⅝" Courthouse Steps

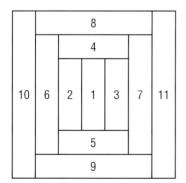

1¾" Courthouse Steps

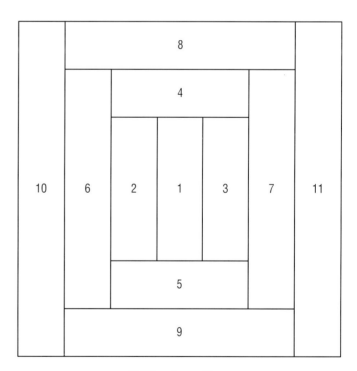

3½" Courthouse Steps

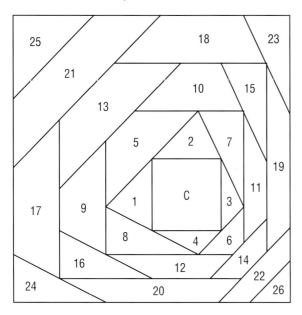

3" Offset Pineapple
Designed by Mary Ann Rush

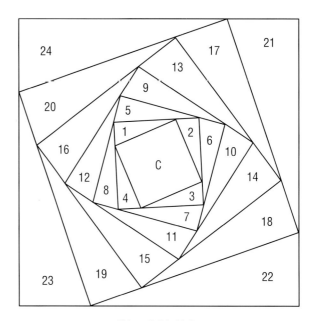

3" Log Cabin Twist

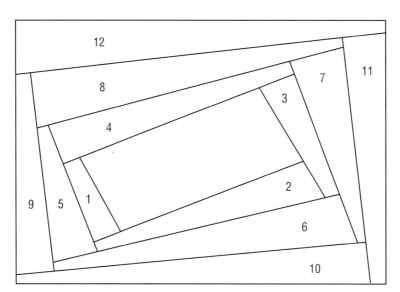

Rectangle Twist
4" x 2¾"

USING DESIGN GRIDS

The ideas suggested in Creating Block Designs with Foundations (pages 64–66), are meant to get your creative juices flowing. To help you get started on your design quest, I have included a series of design grids. There is a grid for each project in the book. Use them to create color and value (black, white, and grays) mock-ups for your projects. You will also find some additional grids to spur your imagination.

To use the grids to your best advantage, place tracing paper or parchment paper over the grid and secure with removable tape. Color on the paper. You can design original variations by coloring a section from one grid, then moving the tracing paper to another grid. There is no need to trace the grid lines; simply color in the areas. This will give you more freedom and time for designing.

It is often helpful to work only in value studies. By coloring light, medium, and dark areas, you can quickly complete multiple sketches. Study these sketches to decide which ones have possibilities and develop those further, using color. You can assign a color to represent a specific fabric in your project to help you zero in on the design.

When a more detailed study is needed before piecing a design or when several fabric choices are being considered, you can make color mock-ups in fabrics. If you are using solid-colored fabric, you can make your mock-up in any size or scale. If you are working in prints, the scale of the print can affect your example if it is not done full size. Large-scale prints look completely different in a 1" triangle than they do in a 4" triangle.

To make a small fabric mock-up in a neat and precise manner:
1. Carefully apply wide masking tape to the wrong side of the fabric.
2. Draw the required log lengths in the desired width (no seam allowances) onto the tape, then cut out, using scissors or a rotary cutter. Many of my students use a small square cutting guide, such as the Bias Square®, and a rotary cutter to cut out log shapes, making it unnecessary to draw the logs on the tape at all.
3. Glue the tape-backed fabric logs to paper by applying glue to the paper, not the tape. It seems to stick better and is less messy. In my color class, we use plastic page protectors to carry and protect our mock-ups—just in case the swatches come unglued.

Don't be afraid to make mistakes or to waste fabric; you have to cut the fabric to make a quilt!

Rail Fence

For 2" and 3" Rail Fence block templates, see page 67.

Quarter-Square Log Cabin

For 3" Quarter-Square Log Cabin block template, see page 68.

Over Under

For 3" Quarter-Square Log Cabin block template, see page 68. For 3" Rail Fence block template, see page 67.

Log Cabin

For 1¾", 2⅝", and 3½" Log Cabin block templates, see page 67.

Offset Log Cabin

For 3" Offset Log Cabin block template, see page 68.

Courthouse Steps

For 1¾", 2⅝", and 3½" Courthouse Steps block template, see page 69.

Collector's Square

For 2½" Collector's Square block template, see page 68.

Friendship Star

For 3" Friendship Star block template, see page 68.

Virginia Reel

For 3" Virginia Reel block template, see page 68.

Small Pineapple

For 2½" Pineapple block template, see page 69.

Large Pineapple

For 3½" Pineapple block template, see page 69.

Small Pineapple without Center

Variation of 2½" Pineapple block template on page 69.

Offset Pineapple

For 3" Offset Pineapple Block template, see page 70.

Log Cabin Twist

For 3" Log Cabin Twist block template, see page 70.

Rectangle Twist

For 4" x 2¾" Rectangle Twist block template, see page 70.

CM Designs
10669 Singleleaf Court
Parker, CO 80134
303-841-5920
*Add-A-Quarter and
Add-An-Eighth rulers*

Co-Motion
2711 East Elvira Road
Tucson, AZ 85706
800-225-4894
*Fabrico multipurpose
craft ink*

Designer's Workshop
PO Box 1026
Duluth, GA 30096
770-667-6900
Patterns

The Electric Quilt Company
419 Gould Street, Suite 2
Bowling Green, OH 43402
800-356-4219
www.wcnet.org/
    ElectricQuiltCo/
*Computer software: Electric
Quilt, Sew Precise!, Sew
Precise! Papers, tear-away
fabric for foundation piecing*

Graphic Expression
1741 Masters Lane
Lexington, KY 40515
606-273-0005
*Easy Tear nonwoven
foundation material,
foundation impression
stencils*

**Gray Wind Publishing/Brenda
Groelz Designs**
308 W US Highway 34
Phillips, NE 68865-2504
24-hour fax: 402-886-2971
E-mail: bgroelz@hamilton.net
*Bird patterns, free color
catalog*

Martingale & Company
PO Box 118
Bothell, WA 98041-0118
800-426-3126
Fax: 425-486-7596
Papers for foundation piecing

MH Designs
288 Appaloosa Court
Hudson, WI 54016
715-549-5395
*Patterns (Send for list of
retail shops in your area.)*

Quilt Arts
4114 Minstrell Lane
Fairfax, VA 22033
*Classes, lectures, and
workshops*

Quilt Direction
330 South Ellison Lane
Waynesboro, VA 22980
540-942-2567
Patterns

Quiltsmith Ltd.
252 Cedar Road
Poquoson, VA 23662-2112
757-868-8073 or 800-982-
    7326
Fax: 757-868-3866
Little wooden iron

Purrfection Artistic Wearables
19618 Canyon Drive
Granite Falls, WA 98252
800-691-4293
*Textile inks; catalog
available*

Rubber Stampede
PO Box 246
Berkeley, CA 94701
800-NEAT FUN
*Inks, fabric inks, stamp
pads, uninked stamp pads
(Ask for the name of a vendor
in your area.)*

**Thee and Me Foundation
Miniatures**
220 Timberlane
South Bend, IN 46615
219-287-2436
*Patterns with multi-use
iron-on foundation transfers*

Thoroughly Modern Minis
PO Box 925
Carpinteria, CA 93014
805-684-6520
www.thoroughlymodernminis.com
*Rubber stamps, stamp pads,
ink, stamp cleaner*

Williamsburg Soap & Candle Co.
7521 Richmond Road
Williamsburg, VA 23188
757-564-3354
*Granny Nanny's quilting
gadgets, printed foundation
papers; limited stamps
available by special order;
mail-order catalog*

Zippy Designs Publishing
RR 1, Box 187M
Newport, VA 24128
888-544-7153
*Easy Piece foundation paper,
patterns*, The Foundation
Piecer Journal

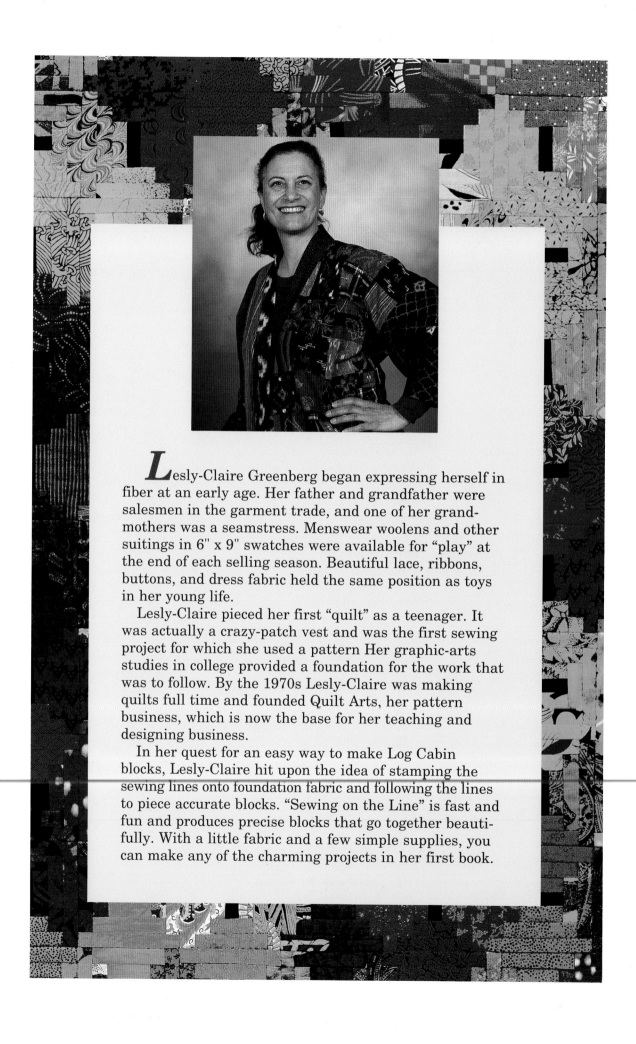

*L*esly-Claire Greenberg began expressing herself in fiber at an early age. Her father and grandfather were salesmen in the garment trade, and one of her grandmothers was a seamstress. Menswear woolens and other suitings in 6" x 9" swatches were available for "play" at the end of each selling season. Beautiful lace, ribbons, buttons, and dress fabric held the same position as toys in her young life.

Lesly-Claire pieced her first "quilt" as a teenager. It was actually a crazy-patch vest and was the first sewing project for which she used a pattern Her graphic-arts studies in college provided a foundation for the work that was to follow. By the 1970s Lesly-Claire was making quilts full time and founded Quilt Arts, her pattern business, which is now the base for her teaching and designing business.

In her quest for an easy way to make Log Cabin blocks, Lesly-Claire hit upon the idea of stamping the sewing lines onto foundation fabric and following the lines to piece accurate blocks. "Sewing on the Line" is fast and fun and produces precise blocks that go together beautifully. With a little fabric and a few simple supplies, you can make any of the charming projects in her first book.